HEARD *and* OVERHEARD

JAMES W. SYMINGTON

HEARD *and* OVERHEARD

Words Wise (and Otherwise) with
Politicians, Statesmen, and Real People

Washington, D.C.

First edition

Printed in the United States of America

Library of Congress Control Number: 2015933902
ISBN 978-0-9915047-0-1 hardcover (alk. paper)
ISBN 978-0-9864353-3-1 trade paperback (alk. paper)

An imprint of New Academia Publishing

New Academia Publishing
P.O. Box 27420, Washington, DC 20038-7420
info@newacademia.com – www.newacademia.com

POSTERITY PRESS
Posterity Press, Inc.
P.O. Box 71002, Chevy Chase, MD 20813-1002
Publisher@PosterityPres.com – www.PosterityPress.com

To Sylvia

CONTENTS

James W. Symington reviews the Presidential Honor Guard.

LISTEN UP!

Foreword by Christopher Buckley

I suppose we're all familiar with the line, "And they say that chivalry is dead!" It is, of course, delivered in an ironic tone, by way of affirming the negative, namely that chivalry is not only dead, but long dead. Well, dear reader, I have news for you: As long as Jimmy Symington, author of this marvelous collection of anecdotes and stories, remains alive—and may he remain alive for many years—chivalry is *not* dead.

Jimmy, or as he is more technically known (drum roll, please), The Honorable James Wadsworth Symington, is a Platonic Ideal of The Gentleman. He is also, more to the point, one of the best storytellers in the world, a distinction he shares with his fellow Missourian, Mr. Mark Twain.

I've known Jimmy for three decades or more. And having spent many magical hours in his company, and that of his beautiful and in every way delightful wife, Sylvia, I imagined I had heard most of his stories, culled from an eventful lifetime. But as I read this book, chuckling and marveling as I went, I soon realized that, as the saying goes, I didn't know the half of it.

Been there, done that. Jimmy Symington is a WASP Forrest Gump (only smarter, indeed, a Yale man.) You name it, he was there. The man has had more lives than a cat; more phases than Madonna.

His maternal great-grandfather John Hay was (among other things) private secretary to Abraham Lincoln. His paternal great-

Troubadour Symington, the US chief of protocol, takes center stage at a reception for young diplomats at the State Department in 1967.

grandfather was aide-de-camp to a Confederate general by the name of George Pickett. Jimmy himself was a U.S. Marine at the tail end of World War II. At Yale he was a member of the fabled singing group, The Whiffenpoofs. He played at the nightclub in the Sherry-Netherland Hotel while getting his law degree at Columbia. (One night after performing, he was asked to stop by the table of Cecil Beaton and Greta Garbo, who paid him a breathy compliment to which he could respond only—not forgetting his manners—"Thank you, ma'am.") He was at the 1960 Democratic convention where his father, Senator Stuart Symington, came within a whisker of being tapped as John Kennedy's vice presidential candidate. Katharine Hepburn called Stuart: "Handsomest man in any room." His son, I can report, is a close second.

Jimmy worked as an aide to Attorney General Robert Kennedy during the Cuban Missile Crisis. He was assistant to the Ambassador to the Court of St. James's, John Hay "Jock" Whitney in which capacity he was called on to serenade the Queen of England—and prisoners at Her Majesty's largest prison, Wandsworth. He was appointed Chief of Protocol by Lyndon Johnson, which job produced some of the funniest stories in here.

He was for four terms a U.S. Congressman from the aforementioned great state of Missouri (pronounced "Missoura"), which makes him a certified, one hundred percent Americano. Well, his resume goes on and on but I'm going to stop there because it's giving me carpal tunnel just putting this much down. Suffice to say that this extraordinarily varied *curriculum vitae* has left him with more stories to tell than the Arabian raconteur Scheherazade rattles off in her *Thousand And One Nights*. And though that is a great book indeed, trust me: Jimmy's is funnier.

Foreword

But this is not just a collection of amusing stories. We find him confronting General Westmoreland over his request for another 100,000 troops in Vietnam; and asking Werner Von Braun, father of the Nazi's V-1 and V-2 buzz bombs, if he believes in God; and being handed a preview copy of the Warren Commission Report into JFK's assassination and being asked by Abe Fortas if he can "find any holes" in it.

Reading this book is like spending time with a fascinating and mesmerizing old friend. I've been privileged to be his friend, and our country has been privileged to have him as one of its premier citizens. When God made Jimmy Symington, he didn't do anything else that day.

SOUND BITES FOR HISTORY—A SAMPLER

Rapporteur's Note

Not another memoir by another elder statesman, this is an anthology of remarks, statements, credos, assertions, declarations, pronouncements, asides and bon mots, the verbal gleanings of four score years and counting. Over a lifetime, certain comments, expressions and fragments of conversation caught my ear and stuck. Ranging from doggerel to prayer, these remarks fashioned the boundaries of one man's examined world. The best of what I have heard and overheard follows in an opening sampler and three collections that resonate distinct realms: the parochial arena of politics and politicians; the larger world of foreign affairs and diplomacy; and, closer to home, out of the limelight. All that said, here's to listening.

—J.W.S.

"Yes Ma'am, But Wait 'Til You See the Judge"

My Grandfather Symington served as chief judge on the Baltimore City Supreme Court in the 1920s and liked to top off his day with a drink—the caveats of Prohibition notwithstanding. As president of Baltimore's white-shoe Maryland Club, he would indulge this penchant in the company of the club steward, William Marshall.

On one occasion Grandpa imbibed enough to diminish his motor skills and accepted his drinking partner's offer to drive him home. On arrival the steward, himself somewhat the worse for wear, mounted the front steps and rang the bell. My Grandma opened the door, and taking in the caller's appearance, declared,

Symington's boss, Attorney General Robert Kennedy, stands between
his brother the President and FBI Director J. Edgar Hoover in 1961.

"Why Mr. Marshall, you're a disgrace." "Yes Ma'am," replied Mr. Marshall with his unfailing dignity. "But wait till you see the judge."

These events were related to me half a century after the fact in a hearty account by Mr. Marshall's son, Thurgood, in his chambers at the United States Supreme Court.

"Unfit to Preach"

One of my early missions as administrative assistant to Attorney General Robert Kennedy was to pay a courtesy call on the Director of the FBI, J. Edgar Hoover—not at Bob's request to be sure (the two were never close) but at the insistence of my father who considered it a prudent initiative. I first checked with Hoover's designated envoy to Bob's office, the natty, soft-spoken and discreet Courtney Evans, who thoughtfully briefed me on protocol in the FBI's precincts within the Justice Department. (This was before the Bureau got its own headquarters on Pennsylvania Avenue, the J. Edgar Hoover Building in the "Brutish" modernist style, which took twelve years to build and cost over twice its initial budget.) Dark suits were the rule, with somber ties; no sport coats or flashy neckwear. According to Evans, should an agent be reported "out of uniform," Hoover would attribute the lapse to a temporary absence of understanding, deriving perhaps from a form of mental illness.

Fortified with this useful information, I secured an appointment, and in my Sunday best, called on the Director. Receiving me warmly, he proceeded to relate how he had captured a certain Louis "Lepke" Buchalter who had fallen afoul of the law as kingpin of the organization known as Murder, Inc. This charming introductory reminiscence—of an event thirty-four years earlier—was followed by a sudden and totally unexpected tirade against the Reverend Dr. Martin Luther King Jr., an "immoral man" in Mr. Hoover's lights, "unfit to preach to others" and a distinct danger to the Republic. How had Hoover arrived at his novel thesis? Apparently under his orders, a bugging of Reverend King's Washington hotel room had produced information about a liaison with a woman other than his wife. In Mr. Hoover's view this impropriety deprived the Reverend of credibility in matters moral and most certainly disqualified him as a national leader worthy of respect.

Upon these debatable conclusions prudence dictates a seemly silence. Judge not that ye be not judged, as one might quote the only sinless man who has walked the earth—or is ever likely to. Nevertheless, four decades after Dr. King was murdered while on a mission to support municipal workers striking for fair wages, he was honored with the dedication of a monument to his memory on the National Mall. Four decades after Mr. Hoover died, at home, a lifelong bachelor, the headquarters building that bore his name was declared obsolete, unfit for rehabilitation or retrofitting and subject for demolition.

"They Must Draw Their Weapons"

This was the ominous condition that the Governor of Mississippi told the Attorney General of the United States must be imposed. In September 1962 Robert Kennedy had phoned Ross Barnett to inform him that James Meredith, an African-American having met all the requirements for admission to the University of Mississippi, would arrive at the campus to register at a certain date and time, accompanied by U.S. marshals. Governor Barnett pointed out that only the threat of overwhelming federal force could justify the withdrawal of his state troopers from the university entrance where their purpose was to bar Meredith access because of his race. Accordingly, Barnett said the marshals "must draw their weapons" to make the point.

"Isn't that a bit dangerous, Governor?" asked Robert Kennedy. "Guns can go off." "Well," said the Governor, "that's how it's got to be." Hanging up the phone, Bob turned and said, "We'll have to think of something else." The eventual strategy centered on an earlier arrival on campus than publicly scheduled. The U.S. marshals would escort Meredith to the Lyceum and remain there with him until his safety could be ensured. Learning of this subterfuge, a crowd of thousands, including both students and outside troublemakers, surrounded the Lyceum and called for Meredith's deliverance into their midst.

From Washington President Kennedy broadcast an appeal for order and compliance with law. To no avail. The cordon of unarmed marshals was bombarded with stones and Molotov cocktails. An ambulance dispatched to rescue a seriously injured marshal was not permitted to enter the area.

The siege was orchestrated under the leadership of retired Army General Edwin Walker. The marshals responded with tear gas in a confrontation that lasted into the night. Ordered by Bob to fly down at once, I arrived in the early morning. The air reeked of tear gas as young soldiers, sent in support of the marshals, patrolled the campus with fixed bayonets to the derisive epithets of a furious crowd of contemporaries. I hope I may never again witness one nineteen-year-old American yell at another, "If you weren't so stupid you wouldn't be in the Army!"

Invited to attend the thirtieth anniversary of the event in 1992, I exchanged memories with Meredith, who had by then gone to work for North Carolina Senator Jesse Helms. Black students served on the university's Student Council, and the student body had elected a black homecoming queen. Change was in the air and on the ground.

"Going Camping?"

The Cuban Missile Crisis of October 1962 alarmed us all. More-over, matters were far worse than the public knew.

In the run-up to its worst day President Kennedy's brother, the Attorney General, assigned me, his administrative assistant, to attend a briefing scheduled by General Maxwell Taylor in the Pentagon's Situation Room. With map and pointer, the newly appointed chairman of the Joint Chiefs of Staff outlined an invasion plan that called for the 82nd Airborne Division to take the island in three days at a projected cost of ten thousand American casualties. That said, such an invasion could trigger the outbreak of nuclear war. The U.S. Navy had challenged Russian ships that were nearing Cuba to deliver nuclear warheads for the Soviet-manned missiles already in place. President Kennedy had given Premier Khrushchev twenty-four hours to ponder his alternatives: either proceed and risk war, or retire and face his generals.

Providentially, Khrushchev chose the latter—at considerable political cost. When the Russian ships stopped and turned around, an almost audible sigh of relief swept across the Potomac. Before the matter was resolved, however, I thought it prudent to devise evacuation strategies for my family from our home in Washington. To that end I paid a visit to Sunny Surplus, a downtown emporium of excess and obsolete military equipment, including knapsacks, blankets, water purifiers, canned rations and the like. There I encountered a colleague on a similar mission. "Going camping?" he asked. "Hope not," I replied.

Meanwhile, through both front and back diplomatic channels, apocalypse was avoided by our reciprocal removal of missiles from Turkey (quietly) in exchange for Russia's *adios* from Cuba. Credit for this escape from the brink goes to Khrushchev and to the brothers Kennedy, who chose to respond positively to his initially negotiable overture and to ignore a subsequent hard line message undoubtedly sent to appease Russia's military. The Thanksgiving hymn was never sung with such fervor!

"Oh, *Those* People"

In February 1961, as deputy director of the newly constituted White House office of Food For Peace under George McGovern, I was dispatched to survey the food needs of our neighbors to the south. At my first stop, Caracas, I was described by its newspaper, *El Comercio*, as *"El joven con poco barbe"* (the beardless youth).

It was not long before I became aware of the race and class distinctions that President Kennedy hoped to mitigate through his newly announced Alliance for Progress. A vivid example was provided by an invitation to visit the home of a Peruvian grandee in Lima. We were sitting on his veranda, which overlooked the city as far as the horizon, when he surprised me with the question, "Why are you here?" I explained that my mission was to survey the nutritional needs of the continent. "But why here?" asked my host, "There is no hunger here." Puzzled, I pointed to a tiny blue-painted church atop a distant hill, which I had visited earlier that day. It was the centerpiece of a barrio called Leticia. There youngsters suffering from kwashiorkor (a protein deficiency) were carrying up to their cardboard huts buckets of fetid water they had collected in puddles below. "Oh, *those* people!" he exclaimed. "They've lived like that for centuries!"

The disconnect between my caudillo host's perception and the reality I had just witnessed was too startling to address politely. A conquistadorial attitude toward the Indian majority prevailed in the upper classes of a number (but not all) of the countries I visited. In others a radicalized majority of *mestizos* (people of mixed blood) had either assumed power or were shortly to do so. It was no wonder the Cuban revolution resonated throughout the continent, a condition JFK hoped to head off with his *Alianza para Progreso*.

"Never So Close to War"

The year: 1983. The scene: our living room in Washington's Wesley Heights. Our dinner guests: Soviet Ambassador Dobrynin, U.S. House Speaker Tom Foley, Indiana Congressman Lee Hamilton, Senator Charles McC. Mathias of Maryland, and their wives.

The evening was prompted by President Reagan's casual reference to Russia as the "evil empire," and Ambassador Dobrynin's

Heard and Overheard

mournful reaction, "My work is done here; I shall be leaving." Dobrynin's long tenure in his post had made him Washington's ranking ambassador, dean of the diplomatic corps. We had first met twenty years earlier during the Cuban Missile Crisis. As that drama unfolded, he engaged in a series of meetings with my then boss, Attorney General Robert Kennedy. As Bob's administrative assistant, I would meet Dobrynin in the private elevator and escort him to the office. On one such occasion, we exchanged phonograph records. I was the lucky recipient of Shostakovich's cello sonata featuring Mstislav Rostropovich, with piano accompaniment by the composer. In return for this remarkable keepsake, Dobrynin had to settle for *An Evening on Buford Mountain,* a collection of folk songs I had recorded in Missouri.

In the 1960s, children routinely learned to take cover under their desks during air raid drills simulating a nuclear attack. Dobrynin's comment two decades later in our dining room was a reminder of that perilous time. I had just concluded a toast to the art of diplomacy and to the ambassador's consummate skills in that department when he rose and said as solemnly, "Thank you, Jimmy, for your kind words, but our two countries [have been] never so close to war."

This unsmiling observation brought Sylvia to her feet with an announcement, "Time now for some music." Mrs. Dobrynin went right to the piano and pounded out a Russian military march, which featured her jumping up from the piano stool and pretending to shoot us. Startled, Mac Mathias fell off his chair. There were no other casualties. Sylvia then took her turn at the piano, and the evening concluded with our soothing rendition of the latter-day folksong "Moscow Nights."

"A Good Question"

In October 1966 President Johnson presided over the seven-nation Manila Summit Conference. Its purpose was to brief the heads of state of South Korea, Australia, Malaysia, New Zealand, Singapore, and the Philippines on the conduct of the Vietnam War and to secure their support for its continuance. The briefing was presented by General William Westmoreland, the trim and bemedaled commander of the U.S. forces. A large backdrop map of Southeast Asia enabled him to highlight the contested areas.

With an electronic pointer he directed our attention from one sector to another, pronouncing each in turn secure, and concluding that victory was at hand. The President asked whether there were any questions. There were none. The President, unaccountably to my mind, then asked, "General, is there anything you need?" Westmoreland responded, "Yes, sir, 100,000 more men." Turning to his array of expressionless guests, the President again asked whether there were any questions. Again there were none. The President then thanked the General, adjourned the meeting, shook hands with his colleagues, and, flanked by his security detail, headed for the door.

Attending the meeting as the president's Chief of Protocol, I took the opportunity to approach the dais, where the General was gathering his papers and preparing to exit. Understandably apprehensive, I found my voice and introduced myself.

"Ah, yes," he beamed. "I know your father." "Yes, sir, and I have a question." "What's that?" "Well, sir, if we are doing so well in the

On a happier occasion General Westmorland congratulates Symington on his victory over Sen. Jacob Javits of New York in a charity match.

war, why would we need any more troops, never mind such a large number?"

The General regarded me with a kind of inward gaze and replied, "Son, that's a good question." He then turned on his heel and walked away—a response that literally buckled my knees. Had the question been put by one of the attending heads of state, I wonder to this day what the necessarily more diplomatic answer might have been.

Eight years later, as a member of Congress, I would be closeted with my Wisconsin colleague, Dave Obey, trying to devise a withdrawal policy that would not denigrate the sacrifices of so many young Americans.

"Find Any Holes?"

Abe Fortas, lead partner of the Washington law firm of Arnold, Fortas & Porter, handed me to review—fresh off the press—the voluminous *Warren Commission Report on the Assassination of President John F. Kennedy.* I had become an associate of the firm during the 1960 presidential campaign, then took a leave of absence in 1961 to launch Food For Peace and then to work for Attorney General Robert Kennedy. I had returned to the firm in 1963 and was at my desk when word came of the unspeakable tragedy in Dallas.

Ten months later Fortas, as President Johnson's personal lawyer, had been asked to review the report. Exercising a prerogative conferred upon senior partners with regard to their lowly associates at about the time of the Creation, he passed the book to me, asking that I review it and report back within hours. When I did so, he asked, "Find any holes?"

Detailed and businesslike as it was, from my perspective the report failed to erase reasonable doubts that the cataclysmic event was or even could be attributable to one angry and/or demented expatriate. But the troubled country needed answers fast, and, as importantly, reassuring ones. Of course, what gave the report credibility was not so much its belabored content as the impressive bipartisan composition of its signators: Senators Richard Russell and John Sherman Cooper, House Majority Leader Hale Boggs, Minority Leader Gerald Ford, former Director of the CIA Allen Dulles, and former President of the World Bank John McCloy. Second-guessing that array of giants and their sleuths was certainly over my pay scale, so I reported, "Seems okay."

PART ONE: TALKING POLITICS

Father and son: Senator Stuart Symington and his younger son, Congressman James W. Symington, walk and talk.

THE KENNEDYS

Is He Qualified for the Job?

That was the question implicitly addressed—ten years apart—by both J. Edgar Hoover and Ralph Nader regarding my suitability for government service. When I joined Bob Kennedy's staff as his assistant in 1962, one of the papers on his desk was my FBI report (which he had prudently consulted, before adding me to his team). Since I was already onboard, I assumed the report was at least neutral regarding my suitability for the post. Yet I was understandably tempted to read it, and, having been accorded Top Secret clearance, I gave in to the temptation.

It was embarrassingly glowing. My friends going back to my college days gave sufficiently circumspect responses to save me from the consequences of what they really knew or suspected. Of course the ensuing half century of potential malfeasance may be reflected in an updated version. I avert my gaze.

Ralph Nader and his minions examined me from another perspective, that of a member of Congress. It was in 1972 that Nader invited all members to cooperate with his *Citizens Look at Congress* research project. Cooperation involved allowing his investigators to enter the member's office, go through the books and correspondence, and take the measure of the member's attendance and voting records in committees and on the floor, so as to emerge in a month's time with an evaluation of his or her contribution to the Republic. This did not prove a congenial exercise to most members, but I welcomed it, as I was curious myself to know what I was doing. The twenty-page single-spaced report on my office was so flattering that I hesitated to show it to anyone. While I appreciated the favorable report, approval by the corporate world's Public Enemy No. 1 was hardly calculated to win votes in my conservative district.

Is this a great country or what? That can produce a Hoover and a Nader in the same century!

"I'm Quitting the Church"

In the spring of 1960, John F. Kennedy's presidential campaign team arranged a taping session to record messages by supporters in the Kennedys' Georgetown living room. Senator Estes Kefauver of Tennessee had just given a thirty-second sound bite in praise of the candidate's farm policy. I was preparing to sing my campaign ditty about Vice President Nixon, "Tiptoe through the Issues with Me," when the front door burst open, revealing Jackie Kennedy, radiantly beautiful with an armful of groceries. She stood for a moment gazing on the scene and, seeing a familiar face, cried out, "Jimmy!" I abandoned our little troupe of broadcasters and rushed to greet her.

We had known each other in a simpler time. Her parents and mine were good friends. My first cousin and Yale roommate, Macduff Symington, had dated her during her Vassar College years. John Husted, nephew of my godfather Ellery Husted, was actually engaged to her when she met the dashing young Congressman from Massachusetts who would win her in record time.

We were reminiscing when she startled me with the declaration, "I'm quitting the church." "You're *what?*" "Yes. You have no idea the pressure I'm under." Without exploring the specifics of her concern, I pleaded, "Do the world a favor, and count to

Jacqueline Kennedy Onassis, who first knew Jim in college, shines at a banquet for the elder statesman W. Averell Harriman in 1974.

ten—no, make that a hundred—before doing any such thing." Indeed, I doubt she would have, but she seemed to enjoy watching my reaction.

This streak of mischief surfaced again at her first post-inaugural White House reception, which Sylvia and I attended along with my parents. Spotting me in one of the parlors, the new First Lady suggested that I sing for the crowd. I pointed out that the crowd was dispersed all over the house, and I doubted it could be assembled in one place. Her laughing response, "Chicken!" has haunted me through life. Two reasons: One, it was Jackie who said it. Two, it was true.

"You Had the Railroads"

One of my regular duties was to meet with callers who didn't quite fit in Bob's schedule. In 1963 one such group was composed of wealthy Brazilian students. Their new capital of Brasilia had been built in the heart of the enormous country, far from the vibrant life of coastal Rio de Janeiro.

Two years earlier, as Deputy Director of the Food For Peace program under George McGovern, I had visited the newborn capital on a fact-finding trip through Latin America. I expressed the hope that the students would take the opportunity to explore and develop their hinterland as our pioneers had done a hundred or more years before. All laughed as their leader scoffed, "You Americans had it easy. You had the railroads to take you west."

I pointed out that we took the precaution of settling the West before linking it by rail with the East. First things first.

"He'll Be Wanting to See Me One of These Days"

George Lincoln Rockwell, Commander of the American Nazi Party, was denied a meeting with RFK and had to settle for me. When I entered the waiting room I found him standing, arms folded, by the window. Dark-haired and handsome, he sported a small moustache reminiscent of a certain failed dictator. His two aides were also dressed in full Nazi regalia, complete with swastikas on both shoulders, fine-looking fellows withal in the good old Aryan way—tall, blond, and supremely confident of their importance to the scheme of things. When I explained that the Attorney General's schedule was full, Rockwell scoffed, "No matter, he'll be wanting to see me one of these days." I suggested he not stay up waiting, and they departed single file, their jack-boots echoing down the hallway.

I learned later that Rockwell had been a supporter of Senator Joe McCarthy and a vocal critic of President Eisenhower's intervention in Lebanon. With anti-Semitic views that shaped his philosophy (if that is the right word), he performed what he deemed to be his duties until his assassination by one of his own a few years later.

"Jackie Won't Mind"

In March 1962 President Kennedy hosted a White House gathering of Latin American Ambassadors and American officials to celebrate the first anniversary of his historic initiative, the Alliance For Progress. That morning I received a call from his Chief of Protocol, Angier Biddle Duke, to the effect that the

President wished me to come over and perform my song "Alianza." I rushed home to fetch my guitar, returning just in time for the ceremonial moment.

The President, having motioned me to approach, introduced me to the patient assemblage. Having no strap to hang the instrument around my neck, I looked longingly at a nearby chair where I could put my foot. The chair appeared to have been recently covered in yellow damask by the First Lady. Noting my hesitation, the President smiled: "Go ahead, Jackie won't mind." Thus, flanked by the President, Vice President Johnson, Senator Wayne Morse, Organization of American States Secretary General José Mora, and other worthies, I gingerly placed a toe on the spotless upholstery and delivered the following musical message:

Alianza para el Progreso	*An Alliance for Progress*
Para cada hombre y niño	*For every man and child*
Un gran hermandad marchando	*A great brotherhood marching*
Esperanza en cada Corazón	*Hope in every heart*
En libertad.	*In liberty.*
Alianza para el Progreso	*An Alliance for Progress*
Quiere decir un esfuerzo	*It means a force*
Un esfuerzo grande y confiado	*A great confidant force*
Para ayudar al débil y olvidado.	*To help the weak and forgotten.*
Igualdad.	*Equality.*
Juntos conquistaremos	*Together we will conquer*
Nos enemigos huirán muy pronto	*Our enemies will quickly flee*
Ignorancia, hambre y miedo	*Ignorance, hunger and fear*
Vencidos por los pueblos unidos.	*Conquered by united peoples.*
Seguridad.	*Security.*

Heard and Overheard

Flanked by President Kennedy and Vice President Johnson, Jim sings at the White House event that launched the Alliance for Progress.

Aplaudimos, pues, el Progreso	*Let's cheer, then, this Progress*
Formemos un gran Alianza,	*Let's form a great Alliance*
Un Alianza de esperanza	*An Alliance of hope*
Y ejemplo para el mundo.	*And an example for the world.*
Alianza para el Progreso!	*An Alliance for Progress!*

"He's Just Won the Medal of Honor"

In 1963 I accompanied the Attorney General on a visit to the New York apartment of General Douglas MacArthur. Bob's mission was to recruit the former Supreme Commander of the Allied Powers in Japan, a.k.a. "American Caesar," to chair a commission to review irregularities in the world of professional basketball. Buzzed up by the doorman, we found the door to the General's apartment ajar. Entering, we were treated to the sight of him sitting by the sunlit living-room window, a view that highlighted his Roman profile. When we had taken seats beside him, he opened the conversation with a Civil War reminiscence.

With his flair for the dramatic, he described how his father, as a young Union soldier, had participated in a charge up a hill under withering Confederate fire. Halfway up the hill the Union flag bearer was struck down. Seeing this, MacArthur's father took up the flag and staggered on. On reaching the hillcrest, and weakened by his exertion, he had no defense against the saber being brought down on his head by a Confederate officer. At that moment the officer was blown away by a cannonball. MacArthur's father, still clutching the flag, fell exhausted to the ground. According to an adjutant's report, the Union Commander lifted young MacArthur and handed him gently to an orderly, saying, "Take care of this boy. He's just won the Congressional Medal of Honor."

Footnote: On a summer evening in 1940, I was browsing in my grandfather's library when I came across a collection of World War I anecdotes by American soldiers. One of them recorded the sight encountered in a captured German dugout. It was Captain Douglas MacArthur trying on a German officer's cap and examining himself at all angles in the shattered mirror.

"We're Taking a Walk"

"Meet me at Key Bridge tomorrow at 5 A.M." This was the crisp instruction given to me by Attorney General Kennedy on the evening of February 7, 1963. I said, "Fine, may I ask why?" "We're taking a walk," Bob explained.

Earlier that day he'd had lunch with his brother, the President, and some military folks, one of whom quoted Teddy Roosevelt as saying a soldier should be able to march fifty miles in three days. Bob's terse response, "Why not in *one* day?" won his brother's benign approval. So the die was cast: we were to hike the C&O Canal towpath from Georgetown to the vicinity of Camp David in Frederick County, Maryland, where presumably we might enjoy the hospitality of the presidential guesthouse as a reward.

I didn't think it prudent to tell Bob that Sylvia and I had invited the French Agricultural Attaché Bob de Wilde and his wife, Michelle, to an interminable dinner dance that night. So at 3 A.M. the following morning, after two hours of sleep, I slipped out of bed with insufficient stealth to avoid waking Sylvia, who understandably asked what I was doing. Stuffing some nuts and raisins into my windbreaker, I explained the mission and called for a cab to take me to the rendezvous. There, in a twenty-degree chill, I joined my shivering co-walkers: Bob; Louis Oberdorfer, Assistant Attorney General for Tax Policy; Ed Guthman, Bob's press officer; and his old friend Dave Hackett.

While I had taken the precaution of wearing my old Marine Corps "boondockers," boots laced to the ankle, I was impressed—nay, appalled—by Bob's footwear: thin-soled moccasins that flapped as he walked. Our fifth companion was Bob's faithful dog, Brumus, a 100-pound Newfoundland who probably wished he was back in Bob's office asleep. Having long befriended Brumus, I was not surprised but only troubled by his friendly jumps on me as we made our way along the icy path. One such demonstration of canine affection landed me in the semifrozen canal.

Walking at different paces, the group stretched out considerably in the course of the morning. I passed the time singing old songs to stay awake and was actually in the lead at the twenty-five-mile mark, where we paused, sat down, ate our rations, and contemplated the necessity of continuing. We had already beaten TR's mark. Bob had taken off his moccasins to rest his swollen feet when a helicopter suddenly hovered above us. Landing nearby, it disgorged a posse of reporters and photographers. With a baleful look in their direction, Bob replaced his sodden moccasins, struggled to his feet, and set out again. The others, save for Oberdorfer and me, followed suit. As I recall, Guthman walked another five miles, and Hackett ten, but RFK, to his lasting credit, never stopped until he stumbled into our Camp David cabin some eight hours later—joining his erstwhile fellow hikers for hot cocoa and an exchange of raucous recollections before turning in.

Heard and Overheard

Postscript: Should the gentle reader wonder how the press was alerted, I believe sufficient time has passed to reveal the source. Our friend Lance Lamont, an enterprising freelance journalist, called Sylvia that day to ask my whereabouts. "Oh, he's off with Bob Kennedy on the towpath," she said, an innocent acknowledgment that may be credited with the news coverage and, as a consequence, the public's ensuing respect for Bob's unflinching courage and determination. My chagrin at abandoning him at the halfway mark was only slightly mollified by meeting TR's test by walking to and from the office for two days, a distance of twenty-five miles.

"I Hope I Never Have to Hear That Speech Again"

This was the bemused comment of Senator John F. Kennedy to his friend and mine, the journalist Charles Bartlett, as he replaced me on the dais of the State Convention in Santa Fe, New Mexico, a whistle stop on the presidential campaign trail in 1960. Speaker Sam Rayburn had already addressed the delegates on behalf of his fellow Texan, Senator Lyndon Johnson. New Mexico's Senator Anderson appeared for Senator Humphrey, and as there were no votes expected for my father I had been designated his proxy. Having not a single New Mexico delegate in our camp it seemed best to enjoy the moment with the following presentation:

Mr. Chairman, Senator Kennedy, Senator Anderson, Speaker Rayburn, and would-be delegates to the Democratic National Convention. As the able and distinguished William Shakespeare wrote in his most memorable work, Hiawatha, *"The sins of the fathers are visited on the sons," and I must say mine have over-stayed their leave lately. Looking about, I realize it's an imperti-nence for me to clear my throat, much less speak. Indeed, I'm tempted to ask for a moment's silence for absent friends—and in my case—relatives. It seems incredible, but the fact is I'm here to help my father find work. I confess the Presidency is not neces-sarily the kind of work my brother and I would have chosen for Dad, but you know how fathers are. They have to feel their own way along life's road, and we can only hope to guide and help when we can.*

All seriousness aside, look at the alternatives before you. Since the advent of Alaska, Texas has eyed her neighbors with a more than casual interest—in fact, hunger. A vote for the incomparable Majority Leader of the Senate may well be a vote for annexation. On the other hand, will it be said by historians that the mighty mavericks of New Mexico were meekly corralled by the cowboy from Cape Cod?

Politics aside—an unlikely scenario—if you would like to nomi-nate someone trained and prepared for the job, I have just the fellow for you. Unanimously confirmed six times for posts in President Truman's administration, he has clearly received an unprec-edented seal of approval from the "world's most deliberative body," one with which Presidents must, on occasion, deliberate. As the nation's first Secretary of Air, he had his eye and his hand on our country's vital security needs. Subsequently, as Chairman of the National Security Resources Board, he had a similar overview of the nation's resources, as they related to security.

National security and the economy, not bad places to start when Presidential qualifications are at issue. Meanwhile, we are beset with slogans and quotes of many colors. For example, 'A Time for Greatness' when even a little mediocrity would be an improvement.

Finally, the generation gap that divides me from my father has presented some unique challenges. At a recent Democratic rally, a very sweet lady took me aside and said: "We do wish the Senator could have made it, but it's so nice to have his brother with us, and thank you for coming, Mr. Kennedy." It happened again last night. "Ain't you Jack Kennedy's brother?" I was ready this time. I looked the elderly gentleman in the eye and replied, "Yes sir, but I've switched my support to Stuart Symington of Missouri." And that, folks, is what I hope you will do.

And I thank you.

At the conclusion of Senator Kennedy's subsequent remarks I joined his sturdy subalterns, Kenny O'Donnell and Pierre Salinger, for a drink and some shared reflections on Vice President Nixon.

"The Best and Gentlest of Men"

As we mourned the loss of President Kennedy in 1963 I was reminded of a twilight reflection in the diary of Great Grandpa Hay: "I have now stood by the biers of three assassinated Presidents, [Lincoln, Garfield and McKinley] all the best and gentlest of men. It is a sad and sobering thing."

Were it not for the sturdy constitutions of Theodore Roosevelt and Ronald Reagan, each of whom survived an assassin's bullet, the list would be longer.

"Promises to Keep"

The following remarks were prepared for delivery at a Young Democrats dinner in Arlington, Virginia, on December 20, 1963, an event that was understandably cancelled.

It rained the week of President Kennedy's death. Following the news that could not be believed, there was gentle, intermittent rain, like tears that come before full understanding. Then there was sunshine—like the expression of confidence in the nation's future which President Kennedy would have wanted to see on our faces that sad Monday. In that sunshine the new President spoke to reassure us that such hope and confidence were justified. Then came rain, full and steady, like the outpouring of emotion that could be contained no longer, freshets of love and memory that washed the deepest recesses of our being, and soothed the hurt there.

We have a new President, a strong, gifted, and experienced man. Yet it is difficult to think of John Kennedy as the old President or even the former President. Why was he taken from us? Better to ask: Why was he given to us? His mission may, or may not, be more fully understood by historians to come. But I think it was to arrest decay. I do not mean this in a partisan way. But discernible in our system, and our attitudes toward that system, its goals, and toward each other, was a kind of soft indifference at the edges and deterioration at the center. The instinct for survival, however, is strong in our body politic. And as one, half suffocated by fumes, reaches to open a window, this Republic lifted the groaning sash of its conscience and cried for help.

President Kennedy talks food policy with US diplomat Richard Gardner, UN executive B. R. Sen, and the deputy director of Food For Peace.

Great men answer such cries. And John Kennedy answered this one. He came in like fresh air. He administered to our ills with such determination, and such strong medicine, that, like all patients, we soon gained the self-confidence to criticize the doctor. There is nothing more truculent than a patient on the mend. He suddenly knows more about himself and all others similarly afflicted than the entire medical profession. In his impatience to be released from nagging care, he questions first the prescribed routine which seems unnecessarily confining, next the efficiency of the staff, and finally the competence of the doctor.

The man who had diagnosed our sickness over a twenty-year period of devoted research and service—and whom we hired to make us well in 1960—had within three years become the victim of this unconscious ingratitude. The British nation put up with a decade of material austerity. Perhaps it is more difficult to put up with moral austerity; for the kind of spite that is vented on those who counsel "stop smoking" or "stop drinking" was beginning to bitter the cup of the man who had told us to stop hating; who cried out to us over the claims of religious and racial prejudice that a man was a man for all that; and through the veil of our indifference, such things as these: that freedom of the aged from untended suffering was both right and attainable; that the poor and hungry of the world needed our helping hand; that our agricultural surpluses should be considered a blessing, not a curse, in the presence of such people; that a Peace Corps was not child's play but good and rewarding work for the young people of a young nation; that in all things we should respect excellence, and that our communications world should share that respect; that neither race nor religion should cause a man to stumble.

He had much to tell us. How was he to get the whole message across when we were apparently growing tired of listening? We were becoming beguiled again by old pastimes and fretful over the continuing interruption. So this man, who could always laugh at himself and his luck, left us; left us alone with the echo of his appeals reverberating in the hollows of our conscience; left us to rearrange our minds to make room for the shame we felt moving in; left us in a silence, dark and deep, broken only by the gentle memory of his favorite poem, "But I have promises to keep, / And miles to go before I sleep." Left us knowing—as we never knew before—that now we must go those miles alone. And realizing, as we never realized before, that if we are to get there, we must keep those promises ourselves. He, who so relished life, in dying told us that.

CONGRESS

"Congressmen Are People!"

This grudging acknowledgment was made to me in 1967 in the State Department auditorium by a young attaché of the Jordanian Embassy. He and some two hundred of his fellow young diplomats, hailing from one or more of the 114 Embassies at the time, had assembled at my invitation as Chief of Protocol to meet and share an evening with the ten youngest members of Congress: five Republicans and five Democrats. Since their careers were to run parallel through the years, I thought it a good idea for them to become acquainted early on, not only to avoid the possibility that each would stereotype the other but also to lay a good foundation for future encounters. Together they would share some responsibility for a safer, saner world.

I gave each Congressman two minutes to address the crowd as to why, where, and how he got elected, and stressed the importance of not being too earnest. The Republicans, who included Don Rumsfeld and Bill Steiger, and the Democrats, including John Tunney and Frank Brasco, presented themselves in the right spirit and then mixed happily among the saris, turbans, and Western garb of their delighted contemporaries. Bread, I hoped, upon tomorrow's waters.

Vote for What?

On June 22, 1970, during my first term in the House of Representatives, Congress reduced the voting age to eighteen. Given that eighteen-year-old boys were already eligible for the draft, it seemed only reasonable to encourage them and, perforce, their female contemporaries to examine, reflect, and recommend on such issues

51

In a Congressional media studio before its iconic backdrop, Missouri's Representative Symington prepares to broadcast a statement.

as war and other national challenges. With that in mind, I established a Youth Advisory Committee for the Second Congressional District, asking each of the thirty high school principals in my district to nominate a senior to serve on it. Its mission: to examine national issues and present their views to me by way of reports from subcommittees targeting local, state, and foreign affairs. Once a month I would visit with them to go over their conclusions and suggestions. Before graduating, each senior would nominate his or her successor to the committee. It proved to be both enlightening and great fun. Sad to say, it was not continued after I left the House.

"Until of Age to Take Strong Wine"

"No child should see an unclean thing or hear an unseemly word, until of age to take strong wine." As I recall, it was Aristotle who harbored this novel notion. In his day (384–322 B.C.), the average Athenian life span was thirty-five years. Accordingly, adulthood (drinking age) might be presumed to have kicked in at fifteen or thereabouts. Clearly our youngsters today are exposed from the git-go on a daily basis to the influences the old fuddy-duddy decried. At any rate, addressing the problem, if it is one, requires at minimum a candid review of all such baneful influences to which our youngsters are exposed—not indeed with the idea of government censorship, heaven forbid, but voluntarily.

Thus, at my suggestion my Youth Advisory Committee undertook to monitor every TV program for a week and mark the number of violent deaths and injuries over such period on each of the three major networks; that is, of folks untimely ripped from the scene by gun, knife, strangulation, defenestration, poisoning, car crashing, drowning, or any other imaginative dispatch of the innocent before their time. Comparing the imposing totals from all three networks (ABC, NBC, and CBS), and finding them virtually equivalent, we decided to approach the three, assuring them of our undying support for the First Amendment but suggesting, merely as an experiment, mind you, that each might contrive to reduce the portrayal of such mayhem by, say, 10 percent in a test week, and determine whether this sacrifice produced an appreciable decline in advertising revenue. If not, then they might try lopping off another 10 percent, and so on, unless and until an equilibrium in revenue was reached below which it was demonstrably unprofitable to reduce the killings.

I wrote the head offices of each network with this mild recommendation. The replies could have been drafted by the same person. There was no connection, they argued, between the ghastly scenarios they provided and the ongoing level of violent crime in the real world. There was no amount of TV carnage that could be deemed inimical to healthy young minds, public safety, or morals.

So there, Aristotle baby!

"Why Aborigines Don't Sweat"

The causes of this phenomenon were the subject of a $100,000 study, which the National Science Foundation proposed in its 1974 budget request. It evoked derision on the part of Congressman Robert Bauman (R-Md.). Waving the overall budget document in the air, he wondered aloud whether the American people really wanted or needed to know—never mind to pay for—the answer to such absurd inquiries. As manager of the budget bill on the floor of the House of Representatives, I pled temporary ignorance as to the rationale for this particular item but promised to enlighten my colleague and, indeed, Congress on the matter.

Two days later I was able to inform the House that the request did not originate from the Department of Health, Education, and Welfare, nor the State Department nor the Agency for International Development, but from the Defense Department. Apparently our troops in Vietnam's sultry climate were wont to suffer from dehydration and its debilitating effects. And since it was known that Australian Aborigines could go without water for a week or more, the question arose as to whether some enzyme or other, responsible for this phenomenon, could in some way be ingested by or injected into our soldiers. A long shot for sure, but one that deserved a look—especially, one would think, by such hawks as my "good friend" from Maryland. It was not unpleasurable to bring this to his attention at a subsequent session. Although to my knowledge the answer never surfaced, the amount spent to attain it seemed a reasonable component of a trillion-dollar investment in a doomed enterprise.

I also took the occasion to suggest that the National Science Foundation adopt titles for future grant requests which were less likely to provoke ridicule among the philistines.

"Republicans Continue to Win Ballgames"

Among the traditions I encountered in Congress was the annual three-inning baseball game between Democrat and Republican members. On June 17, 1969, the Democrat's team featured, inter alia, Joe Biden of Delaware, Walter Flowers of Alabama, Senator Birch Bayh of Indiana, John Culver of Iowa, Lou Frey of Florida, Senator Joe Tidings of Maryland, and myself at shortstop. The Republicans fielded decathlon winner Bob Mathias of California, Don Riegle of Michigan, and other worthies, but most particularly North Carolina Congressman Wilmer "Vinegar Bend" Mizell, who was just a few years out of the majors as a regular starter for the Pittsburgh Pirates.

Gentle reader, if you have never been at the plate with a big-league pitcher on the mound, you have avoided at least one form of humiliation. Suffice it to say you are a great athlete if you can get the bat off your shoulder by the time the ball has struck the catcher's mitt. So forget it. The best you can do to give the impression of competence is to assume the bunting position and hope the ball might strike the bat by chance. After taking a strike on a pitch I never saw, I adopted this strategy. Miraculously, the second zinger actually hit my bat, a grazing blow that sent it high into the stands behind me. After finishing me off with another fast ball, Mizell, six feet and four inches of menacing geniality, ambled up, towered over me, and said in his Carolina drawl, "You trahd to lay one down on me, didn' ya?"

The following morning, during "minute speeches" before the formal business of the day, I took to the floor to give the following report:

Mr. Speaker, as an ambulatory member of the Democratic baseball team this morning, I rise to congratulate the Republicans on their victory last night, and the fine team they fielded, Wilmer "Vinegar Bend" Mizell and some eight others. Last year we lost by a score of

17 to 1. This year we lost 7 to 2. We have cut them down to size. Even Mr. Mizell struck out only five batters, leaving open what might have occurred had he faced a sixth. I would like to close with two bits of advice to future Democratic batsmen, inasmuch as through trades and drafts we may lose a few. First, on the fast ball I suggest that if you hear the ball hit the catcher's mitt, it is probably fruitless to swing. Second, if you have been standing there for sixty seconds and have not noticed anything, you should walk with dignity back to the dugout. You are out.

Mr. Joelson: *Will the gentleman yield?*

Mr. Symington: *I am glad to yield to the gentleman from New Jersey.*

Mr. Joelson: *I would like to tell the gentleman that tradition changes very slowly here. The Republican Congressional delegation continues to win ball games, and the Democratic Congressional delegation continues to win elections.*

Mr. Symington: *It is a consolation.*

So it was that in a time of turmoil, uncertainty, politics, and Vietnam, we found a moment to laugh at our joint and several infirmities.

Love's Labor Crossed

In 1976 our Washington neighbors Tom and Clover Graham were hosting Clover's imaginative and adventurous Sarah Lawrence classmate Hope Cooke. She had recently separated from her husband, the "Chogyal" (King) of tiny Sikkim as it was taken over by India, and returned to America with her two small children. A condition of her marriage under Sikkim law had been renunciation of her U.S. citizenship. Restoration of same would require a "Special Bill"—a legislative rarity—to be passed by both Houses of Congress. Not an easy undertaking, but one which Senator Mike Mansfield and I were happy to pursue, arguing before our respective colleagues that America should welcome home a good citizen who, in "pursuit of happiness" had been obliged to take a step required by a circumstance that neither she nor her intended could alter. While Mansfield's motion was adopted in the Senate, the best I could achieve in the House was the conferral of "permanent resident" status. In any case I believe America is fortunate to have this lovely lady back in the fold.

"Trust Me, ... Mr. Chairman"

The 1976 Viking unmanned landing on Mars had been long in planning. As chairman of the Applications and Technology Subcommittee of the House Committee on Science and Technology, I was charged with monitoring the progress of this most adventurous of NASA's unmanned space probes. Needless to say, my background in law and literature did not fit me to make reliable independent judgments on matters beyond my comprehension (an impressive collection). Moreover, committees such as mine more often than not consisted of members equally devoid of the expertise required to make informed decisions.

Thus we relied on our congressional staffs, presumably prepared by relevant education, training, and experience, to make the members appear intelligent and informed, particularly with respect to arcane questions they likely never confronted

Heard and Overheard

The chairman of the Subcommittee on Science, Research, and Technology takes a spin on Capitol Hill in an experimental car, circa 1970.

prior to their elections. This may be less the case in committees that deal with foreign policy, health, justice, and taxation, where the average member, with or without justification, deems himself sufficiently expert to proceed without counseling. Science does not fall into that happy category. If I am not mistaken, there was but one fully fledged scientist in Congress during my eight years. He was Mike McCormack of the state of Washington. Yet Mike's proficiency in physics and chemistry did not qualify him to lecture on all other scientific fields—other than to uphold the scientific method as a useful guide to truth.

Thus it was that the vast majority of my fellow members on the subcommittee did not deem it worthwhile to attend lengthy sessions of testimony that was beyond their comprehension and to which they could assign a staffer to attend and report anything of interest. As chairman, however, I had no place to hide and no excuse for absenting myself from these heady discussions. Therefore I was alone in addressing the question of whether or not to proceed with the Viking project. The question arose in light of its principal goal, which was to determine whether life existed on Mars, ever did exist, or ever could exist in the future on that distant, barren, pockmarked, and relatively inhospitable planet.

A goodly sum of millions had been appropriated to prepare the project. Millions more would be needed to complete it. It was that second round of investment that was brought into question by the apparent malfunction of the apparatus designed to be deposited on Mars and equipped to test its soil for vestiges of life or the promise of it. We had already proved we could *reach* Mars. Here was the chance to *learn* something about the Red Planet.

Heard and Overheard

A launch date had been set in the confidence that this "life finder" would be raring to go upon landing. But for some reason its delicate equipment did not respond to the tests it had to pass before being placed on the rocket. This occasioned the invitation by Rocco Petrone, project manager, to fly me to the TRW Systems plant in Los Angeles to inspect it personally, with an eye to being convinced that, once launched and landed, it would do its job. I recall examining the device, which was about the size of a typewriter, and being impressed by its alleged capacity to gather moon dust in an ingenious claw and subject it to analysis.

In order to make the originally prescribed launch date, it had to be placed, ready or not, on the launch vehicle within a couple of weeks. Should the launch be scrubbed for want of confidence in the outcome, a new launch date would have to be set when Mars and Earth were once again in the proper conjunction for the trip—a matter of some years hence. Such delay was projected to cost, as I recall, another $2 billion. So—it was either go now and risk total failure for $2 billion, or wait a few years and try again with another $2 billion. As I stood stroking my chin and studiously examining this odd contraption, Rocco whispered in my ear, "Mr. Chairman, it's going to work, trust me." Accordingly, I took the congressional way out, which was to stand aside and let nature and fortune take their respective courses.

I hope I may be excused for being glued to our TV set the night of the scheduled Mars landing. If it failed and scapegoats were sought, I would have been front and center among them: "Symington authorized a boondoggle and has set the taxpayer back a couple of billion bucks." As the moment drew near, the vehicle's doughty camera pictured the up-rushing Martian soil, the dust-producing bump of the landing, and, praise be, the deployment of our dear little life searcher. But what? The mechanical arm designed to shovel Martian soil into the device seemed to be caught. It was stuck. Disaster! That is, until some clever engineer from a distance of 90 million miles managed to free it. The soil thus collected supported NASA's conclusion that Mars was devoid of life as we know it, at least for the present. More recent examinations of its frozen waters have renewed the inquiry. But I am no longer on the hot seat.

"What Am I Going to Do with This Guy?"

One of the joys of serving in Congress was doing so under the leadership and tutelage of Speaker Thomas P. "Tip" O'Neill. Larger than life, and possessed of a heartily positive disposition, he ruled our roost with a kind but powerful Hibernian hand. With his fondness for Irish ballads, he would assign me a command performance of "Danny Boy" for him and his staff on St. Patrick's Day. The habit has continued through some twenty annual banquets of the Friendly Sons of St. Patrick.

A visit with Tip in early 1981 produced the following confidence: A day or so after his inauguration, President Reagan reached him by phone to say, "Tip, Nancy and I were wondering if you and Millie could join us for a little supper tonight." The O'Neills arrived at the appointed hour and, according to Tip, spent a delightful evening of reminiscence so affecting that Tip confided in me, "Jimmy, what am I going to do with this guy?" As I recall, there was not a word of substantial contention exchanged between

Heard and Overheard

these two "Irishmen" from opposite parties for the remainder of their joint service.

"In the lilt of Irish laughter," as the song goes, the nation's business was done.

An Ingrate Dane

My relationships with the canine community have been uniformly positive with one exception: C-5, the Great Dane belonging to my friend and fellow Congressman Andy Jacobs of Indiana. Andy and I officed next door to each other in the Longworth House Office Building (named, as are the Cannon and Rayburn Buildings, for a former Speaker of the House). Andy, a dedicated critic of military overruns, called his beloved dog C-5 because he grew as uncontrollably as the cost of that celebrated military transport plane.

Andy kept him tied up by the door to his inner office so he could not roam the halls. It was my custom, when passing Andy's office, to poke my head in to exchange pleasantries with the girl at the reception desk. Tethered to a desk in the rear, C-5 would observe these brief intrusions with keen interest. One evening, having worked late to complete the talk I had prepared to give that night in St. Louis, I was running past Andy's office headed for the elevator to catch the plane. Andy's secretary had taken the occasion to release him at that very moment. It was then that I was to share the experience of mailmen, who seldom enter houses but hover a moment by the front door, rendering them likely targets of turf-protecting pooches that, unless restrained, would chase them back to their trucks. In any event, C-5, seeing his chance, lumbered after me with an unkind expression on his face. Dog lover that I am, I extended a friendly left hand, palm up, to welcome my canine companion. C-5 responded by sinking his fangs into the hand, puncturing it, according to the House doctor, in six places. I must have taken umbrage at this unprovoked hostility as I struck him on the snout with, as you might imagine, the other hand. He shrank back and crouched, undoubtedly prepared to resume the unequal contest, when Andy's secretary came on the scene, scolded him, and led him away. When bandaged up, I went home and called my St. Louis hosts, the American Chemical Society, to advise them that, with their permission, I would be giving my talk by telephone into a loudspeaker.

Andy was defeated at the polls that year, so it was not until his reelection two years hence that we would reunite to serve the causes of District, Nation, and Mankind. No sooner had the new Congress reorganized than Andy invited me to his office for what he termed an overdue reconciliation between his good friend, the Congressman, and his best friend, the dog. Nor was this reunion to be quiet or private. Andy had assembled his entire staff, plus press and television, to witness the event.

In this festive atmosphere he retrieved C-5 from his inner office and led him proudly by leash to my side. "C-5 wants to apologize," said Andy expansively. "Here, take this dog biscuit and give it to him." I did so in full confidence that the gesture would usher in a new era of mutual trust and affection. Indeed, C-5 nibbled the biscuit from my fingers as daintily as one could wish. He then lunged for my throat. Fortunately, the leash tightened, and he could only reach my chest. Even more fortunately, I was wearing an English tweed jacket I'd inherited from my great uncle Fletcher Harper, who, as Master of the Orange County Hunt, had worn it unscathed through the thickets of Virginia. The result, as later verified, was merely a tender bruise the size of a softball.

Andy, as you might expect, was chagrined at this turn of events. I told him I was fine but had regretfully concluded that C-5 needed to see a psychiatrist. All was forgiven and well nigh forgotten when, months later, C-5 menaced Andy's long-suffering secretary and had to be put down.

"This Could Get You in *Real* Trouble"

Drugs and alcohol continue to provide challenges to mankind and its governance. Human beings are understandably partial to substances that, ingested or injected, relieve pain, moderate frustration, render disappointment bearable, and make any given moment pleasurable as we understand that notion. Employed with discretion and a time-tested appreciation of the consequences of overindulgence, drugs and alcohol have achieved an uneasy truce with the human race.

With respect to alcohol, the truce was broken in the United States in 1920 by the enactment of the Eighteenth Amendment to the Constitution and the ensuing Volstead Act, a legislative overreach as brazen as that of the Viking King Canute, whose legendary command to the tides to recede was deemed responsible for the phenomenon by credulous followers. Thus the corrective Twenty-first Amendment of 1933, albeit welcomed with unseemly enthusiasm in some quarters, constituted a victory of experience over hope.

Congressmen Ichord, Bevill, Symington, and Spence practice the
martial art of Tai Kwan Do in a Capitol gym with Coach Jhoon Rhee.

While "happy days" will never be the lot of drug addicts, our experience with Prohibition does contain useful lessons, not the least of which was expressed by my anti-prohibition grandfather, Senator Wadsworth, a "wet" whose position was shaped by his conviction that "Americans will never submit to sumptuary laws." With respect to narcotics, there was little legislative response until the Harrison Act of 1914, which forbade their cultivation, sale, and use. The nation's prior complacent attitude was reflected in the lighthearted popular song: "Cocaine Bill and Morphine Sue, / Strollin' down the avenue two by two, / Hey babe, wontcha have a little sniff on me." At that time drug usage in the United States was in its infancy. Likewise the crimes incident to it.

Little note was taken of Britain's experience and relevant laws. Thousands of British veterans of the First World War returned addicted to the morphine administered to alleviate pain. They were not denied the substance but provided it via doctors' prescriptions prepared after a medical determination of their patients' levels of addiction. A form of this "maintenance" continues today, despite the inevitable advantages taken by criminal elements. Nevertheless, the addiction rate in Britain would appear to have remained at a manageable level, while ours, under the controlling regimen and underlying law, has risen geometrically. Roughly 50 percent of the U.S. prison population consists of individuals who have fallen afoul of our drug laws. Question: Might there be another approach that could at least limit the mayhem committed, both in the United States and supplier countries, by those who engage in and compete for the illegal market of supply to our addict population? It is a question worth asking. The subject, however, does not lend itself to reasoned dialogue.

I learned this in my unsuccessful race for the Senate in 1976. Having examined the matter over the eight years of my congressional service, I had come to the conclusion that our drug laws, passed as they were in the confidence that they would diminish addiction and the criminality supporting it, had achieved the opposite effect. As a member of the House Subcommittee on Health and Environment, I traveled the country, interviewing addicts, doctors, prison officials, and leaders in law enforcement. Regrettably, from a political perspective, I should not have looked. For I learned that once an individual crossed the threshold of addiction he could rarely be withdrawn from it. Accordingly, he or she would likely break any law passed to forbid it.

My recommendation was that experimental, federally supported state clinics be established in a few locations where the sale and use of drugs appeared to dominate the crime scene. Addicts who had not yet committed worse crimes than usage could safely repair to such a facility for an examination, to determine the extent of their addiction and, if medically warranted, to receive treatment that could well include the provision in safe clinical conditions of the banned substance. Positive results on the crime scene could warrant cautious expansion of the program.

The stout defenders of public morality in and out of office dealt with this idea in summary fashion. Unsurprisingly, the letters I preferred were from those observers who agreed with the concept, including some judges, police officers, and widows of officers slain in crossfire. The quest still continues for an appropriate and effective solution. A population count of persons incarcerated in our federal and state prisons for crimes related to drug addiction should stimulate some degree of rational response, but I'm not counting on it.

One paradox distinguishes this issue from all others. It unites the fervor of both the "good" guys and the "bad" guys in common cause against rationality. The good guys shrink from the notion of providing a drug of choice or an effective substitute to a confirmed addict. The bad guys are appalled at the notion of losing the business.

The latter phenomenon may have characterized my odd encounter at a Kansas City Democratic rally in 1976. Three somber fellows in coat and tie took me to one side to question my position. "This could get you in a lot of trouble," said one of them. "Tell me about it," I laughed. "No," said the fellow. Eyes narrowing, he continued, "*Real* trouble!" I was trying to figure his meaning when my Kansas City campaign manager, Lonnie Shalton, pulled me aside, saying, "Get away from these guys!" "Why?" I asked. "They're linked to the Mafia," said Shalton, as he hauled me into more conventional company.

"Not a Thing, Mr. Chairman"

In 1992 the Columbus Quincentenary Jubilee Commission solicited suggestions for novel ways to celebrate the Admiral of the Ocean Sea's historic voyage. As a former Congressman and chairman of the House Subcommittee on Science and Technology, I suggested a "cosmic regatta" of solar sails dispatched to the nearest planet of interest, Mars. We would fund three winning designs named Niña, Pinta, and Santa María: one from

Europe, whence Columbus set sail; one from America, where he landed; and one from Asia, where he thought he was going.

We scheduled a conference to that end in Washington's Carnegie Institution. Gathered to present their ideas for construction of such sails were academicians and students from Canada, China, England, France, Russia, and the United States. They did so by projecting their versions on a large screen. I had already received NASA Director Jim Fletcher's pledge not of funding, to be sure, but of tracking station support along the way. I also received the encouragement of the National Science Foundation and the National Academy of Sciences. With the approved designs in hand, an estimated $2 million was all we needed to launch the project. This is where politics (as on other occasions) got in the way of progress.

A Miami-based Cuban American businessman who had contributed financially to Florida's Republican establishment had been rewarded by being named director of the Columbus Quincentenary Jubilee Commission. It was a way of expressing appreciation for his help without compromising the prospects of an important agency. The commission itself consisted of good citizens honored by presidential appointment to an entity bearing the name of the illustrious discoverer. They could be expected to rubber-stamp the director's initiatives.

The businessman invested the modest amount of seed money he received at the outset in a handsome brochure featuring his own profile on the cover, superimposed over that of Columbus. This was worrisome. Nevertheless, I was relieved to learn that the Congressional Subcommittee on Appropriations, which would receive our formal request for funding, was chaired by my

Heard and Overheard

old friend and former colleague Bill Alexander of Arkansas. With a glad and hopeful heart, I introduced the newly approved director to the committee, already preparing my happy report to the winning contestants that the estimated $2 million was in hand. Chairman Alexander warmly welcomed him with the words, "What can we do for you?"—a question rarely put to a congressional witness. His answer still wakes me up at night: "Not a thing, Mr. Chairman."

He continued: "I've been a Republican all my life and don't believe we should put projects like this one on the back of the taxpayer. We will raise the funds privately." Alexander looked at me with an expression that conveyed, "Where did you find this guy?" Shrugging my apology, I escorted the triumphant witness to the door and outer hall. "Disappointed you, didn't I?" he said with a grin. "Yes, I confess you did," I replied. Whatever efforts he made to fulfill his expectations, I know not. I only know that not one cent was received for the solar sails, and my sad duty was to cancel the enterprise and inform the contestants accordingly. I understand that the gentleman may have subsequently done prison time for an unrelated initiative.

He Said He'd Blow You Away

My 1976 campaign for the Senate took me to the pleasant community of Webster Groves in St. Louis County, home base of my retired predecessor in Congress, Tom Curtis. Tom had usually campaigned in an open convertible, wearing a white suit. My advisors suggested I do the same. It was rather fun waving to startled passersby, but I wondered why a puffing plainclothes detective found it necessary to run alongside the car, scowling in all directions. When I leaned over to ask, he said, between puffs, that they had received a death threat. I told him if that was the case I would like to trade places with him. At least I'd be a moving target.

Arriving at the bandstand for the speeches, I brought the matter up with the mayor. He explained that, while threatening messages occasionally marked local celebrations, they were normally dismissed as "crank calls." However, one related to my scheduled appearance had the ring of authenticity. Apparently a convincingly God-fearing citizen, aggrieved by my refusal to condemn the Supreme Court decision in *Roe v. Wade*, had called to state in no uncertain terms that he would "blow that baby killer away." The message and manner of its delivery were deemed sufficient to warrant the precautionary protection of the jogging detective. I remember thinking that if I must be taken out at this point of my career, why couldn't it be by a godless communist rather than a good Christian?

"Tell 'Em You're for an Amendment"

This was my father's advice in my 1976 campaign to succeed him in the Senate. Retiring in 1977, he had only a slight brush with the abortion issue. In light of the *Roe v. Wade* Supreme Court decision of 1973, which had authorized abortions without restriction in the first six months of pregnancy, total prohibition would require an amendment to the Constitution. Already in his fourth and final six-year Senate term, he was visited by a deputation of nuns who urged him to denounce the decision. While he declined

Heard and Overheard

to do so, he was certainly put on notice of the importance of the issue to adherents of the Catholic faith, including many of his best friends. Recognizing the looming political implications of the issue he advised me as follows:

"Tell 'em you're for an amendment." "Swell, Dad, what does the amendment say?" "Never mind what it says. You're thinking about it." "You mean I should tell 'em I'm considering some sort of restrictive amendment to the Constitution of the United States which I cannot or will not yet define?" "Yes, that's exactly what I'm saying."

His political instincts were sure. According to the opinion polls, my position cost me 30 percent of the votes off the top, which in turn assured me of placing third in the Democratic primary. This explains my mother's words when asked what she thought about politics. "Not for the queasy," she said.

"A Great Future behind You"

On Tuesday, August 6, 1976, the Missouri electorate put an end to my quest to succeed my father in the U.S. Senate. After the dust had cleared, campaign debts were paid, and supporters thanked, one morning at breakfast my father mused, "Well, Jim, you've got a great future behind you."

SENATOR SYMINGTON

"Off Limits"

In 1948, while serving as Secretary of the Air Force, my father paid a visit to an airbase in Alaska that was the economic mainstay of a nearby town. While touring the base, he was approached by a young black airman with a problem: when he went to the town's principal watering hole and ordered a drink, he would be served promptly enough, but when he had finished and paid up, the bartender would break the empty glass and throw it away—a gesture that appeared to the sensitive young patron to be a sign of disrespect. In any case, Dad took it upon himself to notify the Mayor that if he heard of one more instance of this nature, "I will place your town off limits to every man on this base." The simple directive achieved its purpose.

"My Son Would Be Glad to Go"

Elmira, New York, known as the "gliding capital of America," boasted a 1,000-foot-high bluff that served as a runway for gliders and sailplanes which would be towed past its precipice and released. Gliders were by definition obliged to descend in circles to a safe landing. Relying on periodic currents and updrafts of air, sailplanes can navigate along a "point and return" course of many miles.

My father was invited to the Elmira Air Show in 1948, and among the honored guests was a decorated World War II ace from Texas. Offered a ride on a sailplane he declined, saying, "Ah git nuvus when mah motah sputters, nevah mind not havin' one." The surge of power that an engine provides is reassuring to flyers.

Dad was also offered the opportunity take a sail in the sky. "I don't think so," he said, "but my son would be glad to go."

Not consulted on this rare opportunity, I could see it was expected of me. (I could also see the disparaging headlines, "Air Force Secretary and Son Decline to Fly.") Moreover, it looked like fun. There being no undercarriage, the sailplane is simple to climb aboard. The vehicle is sparse but sufficient, consisting of a fuselage, wings, tail, and cockpit with two instruments on the panel, an altimeter, and a little bubble that slides right and left to indicate attitude as the plane banks. This being a trainer version, there were two cockpits, fore and aft. I occupied the fore. Aloft and free of the tow rope, the pilot worked the rudder and ailerons to maneuver the craft. Once airborne, the sensation is almost dreamlike—no sound but the whisper of wind, and a sense of floating securely on an ocean of air.

All relevant aerodynamic features being then in play, it is easy to understand how Germany could circumvent the post-Versailles restrictions on powered aircraft production in the 1930s. The Third Reich trained a substantial cadre of competent airmen before they ever revved up an engine.

"The West Can Stand on Its Head...."

Among my father's accounts of his Air Force days was that of a meeting of American generals in response to the Soviet blockade of West Berlin. All roads to the old capital were blocked, and the city faced starvation unless it voluntarily accepted incorporation into Soviet-controlled East Germany. The predicament produced an imaginative if costly solution, to wit, the provision of basic needs by air.

One general's memorable suggestion (which was understandably rejected) was the following: secure a terminally ill volunteer in U.S. uniform who, with a rifle across his lap, would squat atop the engine of a supply train as it coursed through East Germany into West Berlin. In this scenario, the Soviet defenders would perceive an armed invader and either fire on him or not. If no shot was fired, the communist blockade would be seen as a failure and be cancelled. However, any shot fired at such a doughty fellow would ignite World War III, a consequence as undesirable from Stalin's view as it was from ours.

The more prudent alternative was the Berlin Airlift, which provided the trapped capital with food and basic supplies such as medicines and even coal for more than a year without the loss of a single plane—an extraordinary achievement. This herculean airlift operation proved in Churchill's words that the West "could stand on its head as long or longer than Joe Stalin could sit in an armchair."

"All He Ever Milked Was a Corporation"

My father's opponent in his first Senate race was Buck Taylor, Attorney General of Missouri. Early in that 1952 Democratic primary campaign, the two were invited to address a gathering of party leaders, committee men, and committee women from each of the state's 114 counties. Fresh from his most recent Washington post as chairman of the Reconstruction Finance Corporation, Dad knew virtually no one in the audience. Taking seats

Mr. and Mrs. Stuart Symington celebrate their fiftieth anniversary outside St. John's Episcopal Church in Washington where they married.

on the stage with their wives, the two were asked who would like to speak first. Turning to Taylor, Dad asked "Are you going to attack me?" "I certainly am," said Taylor. "In that case," said Dad, "you go first."

Taylor took the stand and ripped Dad up one side and down the other, including his lack of farming experience. "Symington never milked anything but a corporation," he said (a good line). Moreover, Dad was an Easterner whose kids went to plush Eastern schools while Taylor's kids played ball and went fishing, Missouri-style. Worse yet, he wasn't even a native of Missouri. Taylor went on in this line for quite a time. My mother, alongside Dad in her summer dress and straw bonnet, was not accustomed to hearing her husband denigrated at such length. She could not suppress a tear. Noticing it, Dad reached over and, without looking at her, simply pressed her hand reassuringly. This simple human gesture sealed Taylor's political fate.

When his own turn came, Dad proceeded without mention of Taylor's charges to dwell on the nation's domestic and foreign needs as he perceived them (communism, corruption, and Korea). He capped his remarks with a telling response to the birthplace charge: "My opponent is a lucky man. Through no decision on his part, he was born here. I *chose* Missouri." At the conclusion of the event, the attendees, one by one, came up to shake his hand and pledge their support.

On another occasion, Taylor held up a magazine photo of Dad totting up his golf score after a round with the Duke of Windsor. "See," said Taylor, "my opponent is a playmate of royalty." Asked for a comment, Dad replied "That's the first time we got any of our

Lend-Lease back,"—hinting that he won a bet with the royal who was a notoriously poor golfer.

President Truman had announced his endorsement of Taylor before my father had declared his intention to run. Good to his word, the President appeared—just once during the campaign—to have his picture taken with Taylor. Privately he was quoted as saying, "Stu Symington has more ability in his little finger than Taylor has in his whole body."

"He's Hanged Hisself!"

Brother Tim and I spent the hottest of Missouri summers as volunteers in our Dad's first campaign for the Senate. In his old Pontiac he would make as many as twenty towns a day, being escorted through each by a designated supporter. I would normally precede him in a vintage sound truck, announcing the projected time of his arrival and plan to address the community at the town center. Our day in the northwest town of Tarkio proved a little different.

With my friend Jerry Oligschlager at the wheel, I would stand with guitar on the truck bed and, between songs, announce over a loudspeaker the imminent arrival of the candidate. Slowly circling the summer-silent streets, we suddenly found ourselves neck and neck with an out-of-control vehicle as it hit a "thank-you-ma'am" (speed bump) and flipped in the air before righting itself and came to rest beside us, engine steaming. Jumping down, I forced open the passenger door and found a beautiful young woman whose white blouse oozed blood. "He shot me," she whispered. The distraught driver, a wiry young fellow in work

Heard and Overheard

clothes, moaned, "She aggravated me." "No excuse," I muttered, holding her head up so she could breathe until an ambulance arrived and medics took over. (She lived.)

A crowd was gathering, when someone yelled, "Look out, he's got a gun!" I could have told them that. In any case, dashing around the car, I grabbed his gun hand. A farmer named Charlie Gibson tackled him as well, and the three of us did a macabre little dance in the middle of the street until I wrested the gun away. At this point a lanky Slim Summerville of a sheriff arrived and, while his deputies cuffed the distraught driver and hauled him away to the lockup, began laboriously taking statements from us. This was in process when a youngster ran up and, between gulps of air, cried, "He's hanged hisself!"

Sure enough, having been placed in a cell with a window to the street, and without the removal of his belt (standard procedure), he had looped it over a rafter and ended his life. My father, oblivious to the event, drove up and asked me why I was not distributing our campaign literature to these "good citizens." A coda to the tragedy was the next day's poorly edited headline in the *St. Louis Post Dispatch*: "Symington's Son Disarms Man Who Shot Former Wife." A fair example of what my old English teacher would call "weak reference."

"I'd Rather Elect a County Sheriff"

An important lesson in politics was delivered early in the campaign. Taking President Truman's advice to "shake a lot of hands," Dad approached an elderly gent in Jefferson City with an amiable salutation: "Hello, sir, I'm Stuart Symington, candidate for the United States Senate, and I hope I might have your support." With a sidelong glance and without breaking his stride, the old fellow muttered, "I'd rather elect a county sheriff any day." Washington, after all, was a long way off. Senators were remote. But an elected sheriff is potentially in your face every day of the week; it was wise to be on his good side. The incident indelibly confirmed Speaker Tip O'Neill's observation, "All politics is local."

"You Sure Got Our Vote"

In July we stopped in the tiny town of Malden, where the temperature was 114 degrees. What ensued made believers of us all. Seeing a group of old fellows rocking on the porch of a rickety general store, Dad, sweltering in his rumpled seersucker suit, walked up and, leaning against the porch railing, confessed that there was nothing he could say or do that would influence them "except possibly make it rain."

No sooner had he spoken than the sky darkened dramatically, thunder rolled, a bolt of lightning streaked across the horizon, and rain came down in torrents. One by one, the old pensioners rose from their rockers to shake his hand. "Mr. Symington," one of them said, "you sure got our vote."

Brother Tim scored a parallel coup in a country barbershop when asked to identify a peculiar-looking animal shoe. Turning the strangely curved iron piece in his hand, he observed, "It's not a horseshoe. It's not a mule shoe. Must be an ox shoe." This correct answer earned murmurs of approbation and, presumably, some votes in hustings where city slickers need not apply.

Heard and Overheard

Bread on the Waters

That summer Dad accepted an invitation to address the black community in segregated St. Louis. As he rose to speak, a voice cried out from the back of the hall: "You any kin to Emily Symington in Baltimore?" "Why, yes," said Dad, "My Mother."

"Folks," cried the voice anew, "that's all we need to know!"

In the early 1900s my grandmother Emily provided food and shelter to indigent Baltimoreans, including the old gent who had put the question.

"The Golf-Playing Crony of a Card-Carrying Communist!"

This was the colorful, alliterative, and fallacious charge leveled at my father by his Senate colleague from Wisconsin, Joe McCarthy. As chairman of a Senate investigations subcommittee and convener of the notorious Army–McCarthy hearings of 1954, McCarthy declared that our government, including the Army, was infiltrated by communists and their sympathizers. He spared no effort to smear committee members and others who challenged the notion. What better way to do so to than to identify them with the enemy?

My father's referenced "crony" was William Sentner, certainly an avowed communist, who was nevertheless the duly appointed business agent of the electrical workers' union at Emerson Electric in 1938, when Dad become the company's president. A *Fortune* magazine article of that year, entitled "The Yale Man and the Communist," detailed their confrontation and Sentner's subsequent cooperation after contract negotiations instituted the hitherto unimagined concept of "profit sharing."

During my father's seven-year stewardship of Emerson Electric, there was not a single union-authorized strike against the company. One day his car was forced off the road by a vintage Cadillac. Emerging to do battle with its aggressive driver, Dad found him to be a heavyset black gentleman, who laughingly approached him, saying, "Mr. Symington, I just wanted to show you what I got with my profit sharing."

Years later in Wisconsin, the state that sent McCarthy to the Senate, I met a newspaper publisher named William T. Evjue who told me how it was that the notorious red-baiter got his start. McCarthy, a Catholic, was having lunch with a couple of priests and said he needed "an issue" to ignite his campaign. "How about Communists in the government?" one of the clergymen suggested.

"Good Boy!"

In the otherwise beautiful spring of 1954, it was impossible to gauge, much less convey, the fear that Senator Joe McCarthy instilled in citizens who might, for one reason or another, deem themselves targets of his freewheeling purge of suspected Communists and so-called fellow travelers in our military. Sylvia and I, newly married, had taken a small apartment on New York's West Side pending my graduation from Columbia Law School. Absorbed as I was in final exams, I could not tear myself away from the daily televised drama that unfolded from the moment the Senate Subcommittee counsel Ray Jenkins's gavel came down to open the hearings called to review McCarthy's charges. I knew

Heard and Overheard

we were witnessing a defining moment in the nation's history, and moreover that my father, as a member of the subcommittee, was a part of it. Much to the chairman's annoyance, he became the subcommittee's principal advocate for fairness and facts. At one point, in response to a McCarthy suggestion, he spoke slowly and deliberately: "Senator, you said something about being afraid. Let me tell you, I am not afraid of you or anything you have to say." *New York Herald Tribune* columnist John Crosby wrote there were few Americans who could or would issue such a challenge to a senator whose name evoked bitter memories of discrimination, intolerance and worse.

One day at the height of the hearings, I went by the neighborhood laundry to pick up some shirts. The elderly Jewish proprietor asked if I were related to "the Senator." "Yes," I said, "he's my Dad." Tears welling, he took my hand in both of his and said, "Good boy! Good boy!"

"Folks Don't Have to Drink"

This confident assertion was made to my father the day after attending a dinner at the home of his colleague, Utah Senator Wallace Bennett. The evening before, anticipating that drinks would not be served by the Mormon teetotaler, my father had invited his fellow guests, including Clark Clifford, for a pre-prandial cocktail or two at his Georgetown home. The subsequent dinner conversation was unusually pleasant and witty. The next morning, Senator Bennett jovially accosted Dad with the hearty comment, "You see, Stuart, folks don't have to drink to enjoy themselves."

This innocent comment predated by some thirty years the expressed philosophy of my friend John O'Connor, attorney husband of Justice Sandra Day O'Connor. "It is true," he acknowledged, "that folks don't have to drink to have a good time, but why take the chance?"

"It's Your Last Chance!"

The 1960 Democratic Convention in Los Angeles had come to order. The roll call of states proceeded to the din of cheers, air horns, and demonstrations punctuated by ovations for each nominee. My brother Tim and I were seated with the Missouri delegation, which was pledged to Dad, a few rows behind Sargent Shriver, the dynamic brother-in-law of John Kennedy, the candidate from Massachusetts. Young and charismatic, JFK was still considered a long shot in the race to beat old pros like Lyndon Johnson and Estes Kefauver. When Missouri's spokesman, Governor Jim Blair, was recognized by convention chairman Sam Rayburn, Sarge leapt to his feet, whirled around, and shouted, "It's your last chance!" His message was that, should Missouri cast its votes for JFK, his nomination would be assured, and, inferentially, Missouri would be rewarded with the vice presidential nomination. As it turned out, the balloting had to proceed alphabetically all the way to the last state, Wyoming, giving that delegation's chairman, Congressman Teno Roncalio, the happy honor of putting Kennedy over the top.

At that point, in light of the solid Southern support Johnson enjoyed, it was not only prudent but appropriate for LBJ to be offered the number two spot on the ticket. But no one thought he

Senator Symington joins President Kennedy in honoring the comedian
Bob Hope, recipient of the Congressional Gold Medal in 1963.

would accept it. Given the animosity that had characterized the Kennedy–Johnson rivalry, it had been assumed that LBJ would prefer to remain in the Senate, where, as majority leader, he would hold a Damoclean sword over the White House legislative agenda. Besides, no one expected the political dynamo and Type A workaholic to accept a post once described as "not worth a bucket of warm spit." However, some weight must be given to Lady Bird Johnson's assessment. LBJ had heart problems, and his wife reportedly believed that serving as vice president would be less stressful than being obliged as majority leader to promote the programs of the young upstart from New England who had stolen his prize. An attempt by Robert Kennedy to persuade LBJ to retain his powerful Senate role only increased the tension between the two fiercely competing camps.

The evening after JFK's nomination, my father called my brother and me to his hotel quarters. Present were our mother, our wives, and close friend and advisor Clark Clifford. Dad told us that he had a decision to make, whether or not to accept the vice presidential spot on the ticket, which Bob Kennedy had understood would be offered. Tim and I said we didn't think he had come all that way to be a candidate for a post of such little importance, and that he should rather continue to invest his views, experience, and energy as a ranking member of the Senate. With a smile Dad turned to Clifford and said, "Clark, what do you think?" We were then treated to a numbing display of the talents of a natural-born advocate.

"Well, boys," said Clifford, putting his fingers together in his contemplative way, "let's see where we are. We've chosen this phenomenal young Irishman to head the Democratic Party as it

Heard and Overheard

goes into the most important election if our lifetime. Right? Yes, and his opponent is Richard Milhous Nixon, correct? Yes, and no question he will be asking Democrats coast to coast to give him a hand, no? Yes. So I'm wondering what more important question could he direct to any Democrat but 'Will you go with me? Will you stand with me, beside me, and help hold high the Democratic standard in this most important election of our time?' And what I hear you boys saying is, 'No, give us something else to do.' Is that what you're saying?"

Silence.

This was the state of play prior to Johnson's acceptance of the number two spot. Indeed, the following morning Sylvia and I turned on the TV to hear Kennedy reveal his choice of running mate. He appeared to have had little sleep, getting the titles wrong as he went over the list of those considered—referring to Governor Loveless of Iowa as "Senator Loveless" and Governor Docking of Kansas as "Senator Docking." Perhaps, with our Dad and Johnson on his mind, the word "Senator" dominated his thinking. The bombshell came after he mentioned Senator Symington as one of those considered. "But," said Kennedy, "in order to fashion the best and strongest ticket to take us to victory this fall, I have chosen our great Senate majority leader, Lyndon Baines Johnson of Texas."

At this point, I suggested to Sylvia that we make for Disneyland, where fantasy ruled unalloyed. There we encountered clusters of delegates wandering about in a daze. "We wanted your Pappy," moaned a huge Mississippian in a broad white cowboy hat. "Didn' want Lyndon to do it, but your Pappy, bein' Missoura and all would've been okay." California delegate Jimmy Roosevelt

Profiles in Congress: Senator Symington and Congressman Symington served for four terms in their respective houses.

stopped us and said, "We thought for sure it was your Pa." Ohio's Governor LaSalle and delegates from a number of other states expressed their puzzlement. But, as we were all to discover, the choice of LBJ was ratified by the very close result.

"Handsomest Man"

Every spring over a period of thirty years (1965–95), I hosted a five-day bachelor gathering of my Washington tennis pals in Boca Grande, Florida. Dubbed the "Bocateers" by residents of that remote and tranquil Gulf Coast island, we were the happy beneficiaries of dinner invitations from local residents, including Arthur Houghton, patriarch of the Houghton family, which included his cousin Amory Jr., a universally respected member of Congress.

Arthur and his family owned Corning Glass and its high-quality Steuben division. One evening he and his beautiful wife, Nina, gave a dinner for six of us at a gathering that included his houseguest and cousin Katharine Hepburn (her middle name was Houghton). Recalling that my father had taken the famous actress to hear my mother sing at the Waldorf Astoria's Rainbow Room back in the late 1930s, I mentioned this to her. Miss Hepburn fixed me with a kindly gaze and said, "Handsomest man in any room."

LAWYERING

"Lawyers, Like Bread, Are Best When Fresh and New"

"Lawyers," wrote Thomas Fuller, are "like bread, best when fresh and new." (For the record, he wrote from the perspective of a seventeenth-century English divine.) I was in that state first in the office of the city counselor of St. Louis, trying cases in police court and preparing opinions for that office. If "experience" as adjudged by Justice Oliver Wendell Holmes, "is the life of the law," mine was enriched at the outset by a series of unforgettable clients, mostly women.

Mrs. Clark's husband had perished when the breathing tube, inserted in his esophagus after a throat cancer operation, fell out. Having spent the better part of the night drinking with friends, he fell asleep in his car after bringing it to rest in his garage. The tube was in his hand. Was this an accident justifying a double indemnity recovery or the predictable consequence of an evening of hell raising? Or was it even, as the insurance company darkly hinted, suicide? The widow's case adduced evidence that her husband would indeed remove the device from time to time to clear it of mucus. On this one occasion, before reinserting it, he succumbed to a possibly alcohol-induced slumber without replacing it. We argued that such a failure, being "unintentional," constituted grounds for recovery for "accidental death." The jury agreed.

A second client, Mrs. Friedlich, had been admitted to the Jewish Hospital in St. Louis to have her baby. At the nurse's suggestion she removed her ring to avoid scratching herself during the procedure. The ring, placed thus in custody of the hospital, unaccountably disappeared—a sad result, particularly since the hospital as a charitable institution enjoyed immunity from tort liability under the current law (since changed). The hospital's distinguished attorney, Norman Bierman, allowed it to be an unfortunate circumstance but not grounds for remuneration owing to the hospital's legal immunity from the consequences of employee negligence or misfeasance. But our complaint did not allege either. Rather, it pointed out that, upon entering the hospital for the procedure, Mrs. Friedlich had signed an agreement to pay in full for its services. One such "service," we modestly averred, was the wise removal of the ring; another would have been its return upon recovery. So the suit was not for wrongdoing (tort) but for breach of contract.

Arriving at the courtroom on the day of the trial, we discovered that the hospital was prepared to pay the agreed cost of $1,200 rather than allow a precedent for contract theory to make an end run around tort as the basis for patient recoveries. Not long afterward, the immunity provision was erased from the books, and hospital insurance bills went through the roof, followed swiftly by those of their patients.

A third case involved the plight of a bereft woman who outlived her long-time "common law" husband. She had begun living with the deceased when "common law" marriages conferred marital rights, as in old England. The custom well served our pioneer days, when women on covered-wagon treks became mothers without benefit of wedlock. The West having been settled (more or less), this common law had long since given way to propriety. Once again, it seemed that the theory of contract, in this case implied contract, might be invoked or, if not, the more durable common-law principle of *in quantum meruit* (as much as deserved). Accordingly, the complaint listed, in support of these alternative counts, the extensive domestic services performed by our client for over thirty years of cooking, cleaning, housekeeping, nursing to health, etc. Unless the estate was prepared to give evidence that not only was the deceased known to be a hopeless cad, but with the plaintiff's knowledge and acquiescence had no intention of compensating her, the court should assess the value of such services and rule in her favor.

In this connection the testimony of the prim and presentable plaintiff included her wistful recollection of the countless times the deceased had said to her, "Don't worry, Mary, I'll always take care of you." Her direct testimony was so affecting that defendant's counsel waived cross examination, clinging confidently to the long-standing termination of common-law marriage rights. As the estate was valued at $30,000, the complaint asked for the entire sum. Indeed, it would amount to a mere $1,000 a year for thirty years of such devoted service. The decedent's two brothers, the named beneficiaries in his will, were sufficiently alarmed at this point to offer our client one third of the monetary estate, plus the couple's little house. Anxious to test my theory of the case in a trial, I asked a senior partner of my firm what we should do about the offer. "Take it and run!" said he, wisely perceiving the likelihood that twelve upright St. Louis citizens, good and true, could not be depended upon to reward a plaintiff who had lived in sin.

"We Can Talk on the Way"

That was the spirited, unauthorized, and certainly unanticipated suggestion of the ambulance driver I was interviewing for a personal injury client of the St. Louis law firm Cobbs, Armstrong, Teasdale & Ross, which I had joined in 1957 after a year in the city counselor's office. Our chat in a garage was interrupted by a phone call. Slamming the phone down, he blurted, "Gotta go. Come along; we can talk on the way!"

While personal injury lawyers are suspected at times of being "ambulance chasers," I know of no other instance in which an attorney was actually invited to ride in an ambulance to the site of an accident. Not one to question authority, I jumped into the passenger seat as the vehicle bolted like a bee-stung filly, siren whooping, and proceeded with minimal heed to lights and traffic until we came upon a convincing scene of mayhem: three vehicles, two rendered crosswise to the traffic by the impact, and the third tilting to one side. The sundry occupants were dazedly drifting about or sitting on the ground. For an instant I harbored the notion that there before me were enough legal fees to support my family for an extended period. Suppressing a momentary impulse to hand out cards, I chalked the incident off to a providentially imposed character test and, as the first squad car arrived, caught a bus back to town.

"Can We Do It?"

There are some of us left who can well recall an America where virtually all places of public accommodation were racially segregated. This was certainly so in Missouri when, in 1954, I entered the practice of law as Assistant City Counselor in St. Louis. In 1955 Mayor Raymond R. Tucker asked his City Counselor, Sam Liberman, for an opinion as to whether the city had the power to enact a public accommodation ordinance requiring all hotels and restaurants licensed by the city to provide equal service to all regardless of race. Among the arguments in opposition was that such an initiative was properly the province of state law, and that cities were powerless to act. But the restraint imposed had less justification in the cases of St. Louis and Kansas City, whose classifications in Missouri law as "home rule charter cities" gave them direct responsibility for their exercise of police powers. "What do you think?" asked Sam. "Can we do it?"

The assignment to prepare a draft opinion required delving into equivalent municipal practices and their legal bases nationwide. The jurisdictional objection that such powers were reserved to the states was obviated by the myriad ordinances in Southern cities that *required* segregation, albeit with the benign complicity of their state governments. The Missouri Constitution, on the other hand, while it did not address that question directly, made it clear in its preamble that the purpose of government was to ensure equal treatment to all under the law.

While there was no controlling precedent, in 1953 the U.S. Supreme Court, with Justice William O. Douglas writing for the majority, had upheld a long dormant post-emancipation Civil War statute that required all places of public accommodation in the federally governed District of Columbia to provide service to all citizens. The defendant in *District of Columbia v. John R. Thompson Co., Inc.* argued that since there was no record of that provision ever being enforced it had virtually ceased to be operative. Douglas explained patiently that this was not the case; a principle of law embedded in a statute did not simply atrophy for want of application. It was an enlightened decision for its time, but at best of mere "persuasive" authority.

Moreover, the St. Louis I came home to with my LL.B. was neither prepared nor inclined to welcome such change. In any case, what would in effect be a civil rights ordinance would most certainly be challenged at the state level.

Acknowledging that such an ordinance would be tested in the Missouri Supreme Court, my draft opinion suggested it would survive that test, if narrowly. The prevailing consensus in St. Louis was reflected in the Board of Aldermen's defeat of the proposal. At this point the Kansas City Human Rights Committee wrote asking for my research. I provided it, and, praise be, the Kansas City Council passed a similar ordinance. It went, as predicted, to the Missouri Supreme Court, which by a vote of five to four upheld it. By then (1961), I had left Missouri. But the answer to Sam's question, so long in coming, was "Yes, we can."

"What Is Golf?"

How can one give a definitive answer to that question without appearing ridiculous? So I learned when the question was put to me by the chairman of the Central Bank of Mongolia over a cup of tea in his modest office in Ulaanbaatar. What occasioned his bewilderment was a suggestion I made in the course of my visit with fellow board members of the Riggs Bank in Washington, D.C. Our mission, under bank chair Joe Allbritton, was to explore business opportunities in the Orient.

Ulaanbaatar, the nation's capital, blossoms like a Shangri-La out of an otherwise bleak Mongolian moonscape that stretches for miles in every direction. Surrounded by peasant dwellings (yurts), it features at its center a majestic Buddhist temple. Saffron-robed monks with shaved heads meander through ornate archways, sharing the cloistered spaces and streets with

Heard and Overheard

randomly wandering yaks. Tinkling bells, dangling from their powerful necks, would announce the approach of these burly bovines. This phenomenon, complemented by the distant howling of wolves at eventide, seemed to diminish the prospects of modernity in this sleepy center of a one-time empire whose conquering pony-borne hordes had swept all the way to Europe.

How to reenergize this patiently somnolent subsistence economy was our challenge. As I gazed on the verdant plains that undulated before us, it occurred to me that they could accommodate a goodly number of golf courses. I'd heard that Japanese golfers, in order to circumvent the prohibitive greens fees in their homeland, were flying all the way to Hawaii for a weekend game—three times farther than the hop to my imagined "Mongolfia." Hence the suggestion that prompted the chairman's reasonable inquiry, "What is golf?" But, aye, that was the rub! By the time I had described with minimal particularity the process of striking a small ball with a stick and then looking for it as a "sport" (one that George Bernard Shaw labeled "a good walk spoiled"), I had lost my audience.

"I Hate to Speak Ill of Anyone, but He Is a Lawyer"

So quipped England's prodigious Samuel Johnson in describing an acquaintance. And in a similar vein, asks the rebel Jack Cade in Shakespeare's *Henry VI, Part 2*, "Is not this a lamentable thing that of the skin of an innocent lamb should be made parchment; that parchment, being scribbled o'er, should undo a man?" "The first thing we do," says Dick the Butcher in the same work, "let's kill all the lawyers."

Of his Utopians, Sir Thomas More wrote, "They have no lawyers among them, for they consider them a sort of people whose profession it is to disguise matters."

Before recognizing the skull he held as that of "poor Yorick," Hamlet speculated, "Why may not that be the skull of a lawyer? Where be his quiddities now, his quillets, his cases, his tenures, and his tricks?"

"Washington would be better off," said Nixon's Secretary of Agriculture Earl Butz, "with a few less smart, young lawyers."

Moreover, some years ago a national poll was taken that measured the level of public respect for the practitioners of the world's various occupations. Near the top were refuse collectors. Near the bottom were lawyers. So what induced me to take up such a maligned profession? Acceptance of the notion that law and order are unlikely to be achieved without lawyer-made orderliness. In Albert Einstein's view, "Our defense is not in armaments, nor in science, nor in going underground.... Our defense is in the law."

Echo More's advice (in the play *A Man for All Seasons*) to Roper, his rebellious son-in-law: "And when the last law was down, and the Devil turned round on you—where would you hide, Roper, the laws all being flat? This country is planted thick with laws from coast to coast—man's laws, not God's—and if you cut them down ... do you really think you could stand upright in the winds that would blow then?"

John Locke put it this way: "Wherever Law ends, Tyranny begins."

For my part the privileges of tyranny should be reserved only to parents of minors.

For forty years Jim served as "Crop Reporter" of the Alfalfa Club,
a unique Washington Institution—longer than any other officer.

"A Lawyer When Needed"

Teaching our course on "Law in Society" at Columbia University was the elegant Professor Elliott Cheatham. Slender and graying, with a soft Southern accent, he was a class favorite. His book *A Lawyer When Needed* emphasized the importance of taking on cases and clients considered anathema by the world at large. Acknowledging that representation of unpopular clients or causes would come at a risk, he maintained that lawyers should nevertheless assume that responsibility.

Thirty years later, the South African government most certainly fell into that category when, at the behest of a South African antiapartheid intermediary, my partner, former Florida Senator George Smathers, and I agreed to represent the country while it shed its raced-based laws in favor of majority rule. Our first assignment was to draft a constitutional structure that would achieve this result. So, while a trifle nerve-wracking, it was not entirely surprising to be informed by the FBI that a midnight raid on the New York offices of the Black Panthers had produced plans to blow up our office. Said plans included a map of the layout and a schedule of our comings and goings. The bureau's only suggestion was to have our firm name removed from the lobby register—a stopgap measure at best. Beyond that we were advised the most likely time frame for such an unwelcome visit would be after 7 P.M., when most of the offices would be closed. Apparently it was thought not to be the intent of the considerate Panthers to take life unnecessarily. Only those who had the misfortune to work late on the wrong night might number among the casualties.

Heard and Overheard

After the passage of a month or so of understandably keen awareness, we were notified that, possibly due to some arrests, the threat had subsided. I confess it was off-putting for staff, clients, and clean-up crews not to be sure they would survive time spent on our premises.

"Developers Are Like *Jaws*"

This was the verdict of my Great-Aunt Harriet Wadsworth Harper, widow of Fletcher Harper, Master of the Orange County Hunt in Virginia for a half century. To her the Virginia Piedmont was sacrosanct. Granddaughter of General James S. Wadsworth, she had taken up riding sidesaddle at the age of five with such determination that, seven years later, she was diagnosed with curvature of the spine. Her prescient doctor's advice: switch to the offside (ride left-handed). She did so, straightened up, and rode on for a half century, mostly through the Piedmont area. As she approached ninety she willed a few acres of her beloved land to my brother Tim and me, admonishing us not to sell to developers who, she said, "like *Jaws*," would gobble every acre all the way to the Blue Ridge Mountains.

At the time of her death, the applicable Virginia law provided that open land could be sold and then divided into home sites of seven acres. As a consequence the Piedmont Environmental Council (PEC) led the move to fend off developers by establishing "scenic easements"—a binding proviso that kept a given tract of land forever open. Such an easement clearly diminished a tract's value. So property owners understandably expected a tax break based on the estimated differential between the value of the land as undeveloped and its value as potentially developable. Curiously, the Internal Revenue Service perceived no appreciable difference between the two valuations. Thus the entire easement program was put on hold until a court determination could be made.

Lawyers for the major landholders, owning thousands of acres, wanted to bundle all their cases together and asked me to join them. To their dismay I preferred to go it alone and took the IRS to the U.S. Tax Court in Washington. Displaying photos of my land with uninterrupted views all the way to the western horizon, I argued that each of the six seven-acre lots that it could accommodate would enjoy that view. I also invited the judge to come and see for himself. He did so and confirmed a handsome differential between the two valuations. The decision saved the easement program, earning me a dandy certificate of commendation from the PEC. I suppose I might have preferred a little help with the legal bill.

"Isn't This Your Signature?"

In 1871 President Ulysses S. Grant expressed his gratitude to Russia's Czar Alexander II for his support in our Civil War by inviting him to send one of his boys on a goodwill trip to the newly reunited States. Alexander chose his fourth son, twenty-one-year-old Grand Duke Alexis, to make what proved to be the most extraordinary visit of its kind in our history. It included an audience with Grant; a demonstration fire drill in New York; dinner in Boston featuring laudatory remarks by poets Whittier, Longfellow, and Oliver Wendell Holmes; visits to some twenty-two cities (including Chicago, where he donated $5,000 to the victims of its historic fire), in most of which he could be depended upon to open a quadrille with the mayor's daughter; a stop in Canada to express sympathy for Albert, Queen Victoria's ailing Prince Consort; a buffalo hunt in Nebraska with Generals Custer and Sheridan and Buffalo Bill Cody, and a final farewell gala in New Orleans, where his figure as "Rex" became the enduring theme of the Mardi Gras parade. Any questions?

In 1996, as chairman of the American-Russian Cultural Cooperation Foundation (ARCCF), my idea was to commemorate the 125th anniversary of this remarkable tour of our resurgent nation and the warm receptions accorded our royal visitor, by inviting the Russian government to select twenty-one twenty-one-year-old Russian men and women to take the same trip to the same destinations, and receive similar hospitality. I had already received assurances from mayors' offices that they would welcome the visitations before I broached the idea with Russia's Cultural Ministry. In response I received a notification that the ministry had referred the project to a private promoter, who proposed, in lieu of students, that Russia would send its Romanov crown jewels for display in our museums, the first time they had ever traveled outside Russia.

This was not my idea. I preferred students to jewels, but beggars can't be choosers; it was either jewels or nothing. Accordingly, I embarked on a perilous undertaking that would define 1996, in the words of Queen Elizabeth II, as my *annus horribilis*. The entity to which the Cultural Ministry seconded its mission was less interested in history than revenue. The contract draft presented was so one-sided I could not sign it. We were dead in the water when I received a call that the treasures had surprisingly arrived in New York and were headed to our first designated venue, Washington's Corcoran Gallery of Art.

Puzzled, I asked for a meeting with ministry representatives. Held in the conference room of a Washington law firm, it brought me and the foundation's attorney, Michael Goldstein, head to head with the visiting ministerial representative and the charming and resourceful promoter who had hijacked our endeavor. I omit names as they would mean little, and they know who they are. At the outset of the meeting, our distinguished guest reached in his pocket and produced with considerable flourish the "agreement" upon which he relied.

"Isn't this your signature?" he asked, with the confidence of a man holding four aces. "Yes." "Well, then, what's the problem?" "The problem is," I said, "that I didn't put it there."

Horrified, he wrenched it from my hands and stuffed it back into his jacket. His friend the promoter, now looking at the ceiling, had failed to apprise him of this bit of chicanery, but both perceptively adjudged that my devotion to the project would prevent me from bringing it to an abrupt conclusion with a charge of forgery and its predictably negative consequences to world peace. Indeed, short of time and options, we agreed to negotiate anew. Meanwhile, as none of the needed proceeds would be in hand until the conclusion of the tour, I managed to secure a personal loan of $400,000 from Washington's Riggs Bank with no security but my hitherto, as I recall, unblemished record. Financially, it was touch and go throughout the tour, until our meager share of the proceeds reached the required sum within a week of the jewels' homeward voyage.

An additional and quite unexpected obstacle to the process arose in the form of a lawsuit filed in Houston by the disgruntled descendants of an American-owned piano manufacturer in Russia, whose plant had been expropriated by the Bolsheviks in the 1930s. As my foundation was named codefendant, and I was its principal source of funds, I was naturally impressed by the amount demanded, to wit, $20 million. Aware of the old adage that a lawyer who represents himself has a fool for a client, I sent the petition to the Washington office of a distinguished Houston firm for advice. The firm apparently deemed the suit of so little merit that it did not warrant response. This music to my ears died down when I received by registered mail a default judgment for the full amount rendered by the federal court in Houston, Judge David Hittner presiding.

I immediately contacted the Russian Embassy to explain the need to have that judgment vacated on its part. I then made a beeline to Houston to testify that the ARCCF was not a partner in the undertaking but merely a facilitator. Satisfied on this point, the Judge dismissed us. He then came down pretty hard on the absent defendant, the government of Russia. Unless also vacated in thirty days, that judgment could warrant the attachment of Russian properties in the United States, including the recently arrived treasures. Fortunately, a provision of law known as the Fulbright Amendment protected foreign nations' cultural objects on U.S. soil pursuant to valid agreements with State Department notification.

Although no attachment would occur, the judgment itself remained in force and required representation on behalf of the Russian government if it were to be overturned. I did my best to explain that our federal government, however motivated, had no power to overturn judgments rendered in our state courts. Alexander II would have understood this concept, but we had missed him by a century. I was then advised by the Embassy that in this case it had the authority but regrettably not the resources to pursue the matter. Time being of the essence, I approached a trusting friend for an additional loan of the $40,000 necessary to secure the services of suitable counsel for Russia.

Meanwhile, the Corcoran Gallery opening, featuring remarks by Vice President Al Gore and Prime Minister Viktor Chernomyrdin, provided an opportunity for the gallant Russian curators to tell me that funds we had earlier sent to compensate their services had not been forwarded to them by our Russian "partners." At the closing of the exhibit the treasures were carefully loaded on the huge van we had hired to take them to the next venue, Houston. As it left the Corcoran it was intercepted by some unmarked cars and conducted onto the walled grounds of the Russian Embassy, where it remained during the next chapter of the saga. The long-suffering Russian museum representatives, having been detained in their hotel by a plainclothes team from an "unknown source," were finally permitted to rejoin their associates in the Embassy. Remember, while no agreement had yet been signed, the pressure to make our Houston opening was sufficiently urgent to justify instant renegotiation even on Russian terms. Desperate measures were in order.

My response was a call to my friend, former congressional colleague, and, more importantly, former President George Herbert Walker Bush. Why vex such an innocent man? I knew that Houston's eminent heart surgeon, Dr. Michael DeBakey, had ministered successfully to Russia's President Boris Yeltsin. I suggested that a good word from the man who may have saved the latter's life might produce the desired result, i.e., the exhibit's release from diplomatic bondage and permission to proceed without further harassment. Arrangements were soon on track, and the van, its contents, and very relieved American driver were on their way to yet another rendezvous with destiny. In the meantime, my hair had turned gray.

"Hardly 'Nuff at All"

As attorneys for the American Horse Council, George Smathers and I were invited to attend a "stirrup cup" gathering before the 1973 Kentucky Derby. A British visitor had stopped the steward who was serving mint juleps to ask how many a person could safely consume. The steward's eyes brightened as he addressed the inquiry. "Well, sir, one is hardly 'nuff. Two is one too many. Three is hardly 'nuff at all."

POLITICS

"I'd Prefer a Majority"

A packed house in St. Louis's Kiel Auditorium greeted the Democratic candidate for President, Adlai E. Stevenson of Illinois, one autumn evening in 1952. Eleanor Roosevelt, the great lady of Democratic politics, was there to introduce him with her signature charm, vigor, and toothy grin. But the handwriting was on the wall as to his chances against the favorite, Dwight D. Eisenhower, the hero of World War II only seven years before. The roar of applause died down as Stevenson reached the podium and produced his notes. In that brief interval, a voice from the rear shouted, "Don't worry, Adlai, all the *thinking* people are with you!" Looking over his glasses, he replied, "I'm terribly sorry; I'd prefer a majority."

The Governor's wry sense of humor surfaced again after the 1956 presidential election. "I think I've missed my calling," he said. "In fact, I've missed it twice."

"A Dog Named George"

The summer of 1972 found me preoccupied with my campaign for reelection to a third term in the House. That same summer witnessed the ill-fated presidential campaign of my esteemed partner in Food For Peace, George McGovern. Having perforce dropped my fellow Missourian, Tom Eagleton, from his ticket owing to revelations about treatments for mental illness, McGovern's welcome in the state was muted. In fact, I was the only office holder willing to be seen with him.

The main event was a planned rally in a large shopping center

111

Stumpin' for Pa: In 1952 young Jim hits the campaign trail for his dad's first bid to represent Missouri in the United States Senate.

in St. Louis County. A stage had been erected that commanded views in all directions. One such caught the keen eye of Senator McGovern, a decorated bomber pilot in the second war to end all wars. It was a giant movie marquee. Visible for miles, it heralded the title of a new movie, *A Dog Named George*. McGovern smiled and said, "Good work, Jim."

"What the President Needs"

By 1973 President Nixon's options were all but exhausted, and talk of impeachment was in the air. One evening at a black tie dinner in Washington's old F Street Club, Henry Kissinger took the opportunity to reflect on the President's plight. "What the President now needs," he intoned, "is an act of love." The embarrassing silence was mercifully broken by Senator Frank Church. "No, indeed," he smiled. "What the President needs is an Act of Congress."

"A Milk Pail between Her Legs"

Since over half of Missouri is rural, it is politic for candidates to identify with that portion of the electorate. A striking instance of this compulsion was the statement by one Lemuel McClimans, who was running for local office in a farming community. To buttress his case for consideration, his campaign materials included the following: "My mother grew up with a milk pail between her legs." Whether this credential carried the day I can't recall, but the image has settled comfortably in my memory.

"One Vote Can Make a Difference"

Addressing the Greater Springfield (Missouri) Press Club in 1974, I read from a letter I had written to President Nixon months earlier; the previous year; he resigned the presidency on August 9, 1974.

... The public is bewildered by a sudden cold indifference to the want of virtue in your closest associates, men you selected and offered up as examples of peerless integrity. The press did not choose these men. You did. Many of them have brought shame on America, on you, on all of us in public life. What can the people do but look to you for some expression of sorrow and righteous indignation, and the application without fear or favor of the swift sword of an outraged president? Not sanctimonious resignations, ambiguous testimonials, bland references to misguided zeal, raucous receptions for replacements, but a stern accounting they asked, a fierce, tenacious, and relentless searching out of every man who did not do his duty as the law directed him to do.

What did they get? First, the assertion of a blanket executive privilege over the entire federal establishment, stretching both into the past and the future. Second, puzzling praise when you spoke of certain resignees, and stranger silence when you should have spoken, as for example when your former Attorney General testified he might consider committing a felony to secure your re-election. This chilling avowal awakened no response from you. Nor did John Ehrlichman's calm observation that Pitt's defense of cottage against King was old-fashioned. It was, indeed, even more old-fashioned than the document which severed us from that

Heard and Overheard

King. That document alleged the King had "obstructed the Administration of Justice." Then, in a flash of time you found it necessary to sacrifice three of the most respected and distinguished men in your government. Your administration has been like an inferno consuming the professional lives of patriots. We look at the shattered careers of men young and old. We look at the blatant subordination of so many great agencies of government to momentary political advantage and evasion of law. Mr. President, is it any wonder the people, or a good part of them, withhold their confidence from you as they contemplate the fallen and see the law dethroned by personal vindictiveness? . . .

It is important now to know what you believe the American people as a whole think of your leadership, and what you believe, in the light of all that has occurred, they should think of it. Within the answer to that question lies the nature and degree of your own inner resolve and the effectiveness of every initiative you take. No one can answer it for you. History will second-guess your judgment. And if you hold the people to a higher regard for your leadership than you yourself think warranted by the events of your tenure, its judgment cannot be favorable. And what would it then be of those of us who allowed your conscience to be the sole determining factor in the great decisions of our time? . . .

Reflection led me to believe that I needn't check my in-box for a reply to that four-month old letter. The significance of the silence was in one sense small. An administration which could pursue privilege, impoundment, and war without a manifest concern for Congress as an institution might not be expected to focus on the communications of individual members. In another sense, the significance was not so small. Through a conjunction of accidents of history, I was a member of what is essentially a grand jury soon to be called to determine if there was probable cause to believe the President has fallen short of the minimal requirements of his office. What vote in a lifetime would be more important? My ancestor, Senator Reverdy Johnson of Maryland, not only cast his vote for acquittal in the impeachment of Andrew Johnson (no relation) but helped persuade a key undecided member, Senator Grimes of Massachusetts, to support the President as well. One vote can make a difference. One member can make a great difference. Andrew Johnson was found not guilty by one vote.

"Sauve Qui Peut"

As a failed Episcopalian, I have great respect, admiration, and gratitude for the Catholic faith and its works on behalf of humanity. Nor have I any better friends on earth than those who subscribe to it. Indeed, until 1973 I could conceive of no political issue that could render me persona non grata in official Catholic circles. Caught off guard that year by the Supreme Court's *Roe v. Wade* decision, I was urged to support its reversal—via Constitutional amendment—by Missouri's clerical hierarchy, from Cardinal Carberry on down to parish priests in my home city of St. Louis. Since I could not in conscience do so, leaflets calling for my defeat were distributed on church grounds. One place of worship held a mass to the same end. I thought that my old friend Bishop Joe McNicholas might offer respite from the barrage of denunciation. As Assistant City Counselor in 1955 I had supported his efforts to

Heard and Overheard

secure publicly financed schoolbooks and transportation for Catholic children. Over a cup of coffee, he said, not unkindly, "Jimmy, I don't even know your opponent, but if he's right on this issue I'm for him 100 percent." It was a chilling reminder that church doctrine would trump the ace of friendship.

A related event was my friend Dick Gephardt's resignation as chairman of my Symington for Senate St. Louis committee just two months before the primary. At a mournful breakfast meeting at Stan and Biggie's restaurant, he revealed that the diocese had warned him of the negative political consequences of supporting my candidacy. As I recall, he said they had put it to him this way: "Resign your chairmanship of the Symington campaign, or you won't get elected to the House." I told Dick I was reminded of the French expression *Sauve qui peut* (Save yourself who can). There was no need to put his budding political career at such risk.

But I knew the consequent loss of my St. Louis base would spell *finis* to my noble quest to save the world as a United States senator. Although not Catholic, Dick did promptly and publicly resign. Elected to the House that fall, he went on to an illustrious political career that culminated in his leadership in Congress and a subsequent praiseworthy campaign for the presidency. Although the latter dictated a strategic shift, or possible return, to the prochoice fold, it enabled him to continue to provide invaluable service to the country across the whole range of national issues.

"The Greatest Thrill in Politics"

"I've been a Republican all my life, and what's more you're the last person I'd ever vote for." This simple declarative sentence was written to me in a bold hand by a woman in my St. Louis County congressional district. She had apparently received a letter that, relying on a faulty list, I had sent and signed, thanking her for attending a ladies' coffee in support of my 1976 Senate race. (When I shared her reply with my Missouri colleague and humorist Bill Hungate, he advised, "Put her down as doubtful.")

Later that month, finding myself in the lady's neighborhood, I decided to stop by her house and apologize for disturbing her peace. I first took the precaution of dropping by a nearby flower shop and buying a dozen red roses. Bouquet in hand, I knocked on her door. It opened violently, revealing a woman of certain years in her bathrobe, curlers in her hair, and a carpet sweeper in hand. Before she could register her annoyance, I told her, roses extended, how truly sorry I was to spoil her day by thanking her for a visit she did not make and for support she did not offer. Her look of fury morphed into one of partial and then full recognition, and she replied, "Heavens! Do come in. The place is a mess, but do come in." We chatted for an hour during which she related the woes that beset her, concluding with a tearful pledge of support. The experience brought to mind a remark my father had once made: "The greatest thrill in politics is making a friend out of an enemy."

With Sylvia beside him, Jim hits the streets of St. Louis as he opens his own first campaign headquarters to run for Congress in 1968.

"A Squirrel in Your Lap"

"Dealing with Cuba," observed my great-grandpa, John Hay, Secretary of State in 1898, "is like trying to conduct a polite conversation with a squirrel on your lap." He was reflecting on the complexities that would mark our relations with that mercurial country from the inception of its independence—which we engineered. After a couple of false starts in our attempt to establish a democratic form of government following the ouster of Spanish rule, we left the island paradise to its own devices.

With no experience in self-governance, the islanders allowed themselves to fall into the hands of a series of self-seeking caudillos, with the one brief exception of the patriot José Martí, who died before he could achieve his reforms. The last of the caudillo class was Fulgencio Batista. The U.S. decision to deny him combat aircraft and other aid guaranteed victory for the guerilla forces under Fidel Castro. Early hopes that Fidel might introduce democratic rule were dashed by his emerging *personalismo* approach to governance and drift into communism.

After the subsequent stormy passage of years, including the Bay of Pigs debacle and the Cuban Missile Crisis, I thought it time to take a better look. In 1992, in concert with my fellow former Congressman, Republican Lou Frey of Florida, I initiated a two-week visit to Cuba by a six-man bipartisan delegation of former members of Congress. We began our preparation by soliciting the advice and guidance of the leadership of the Cuban émigré community. Understandably opposed to the government they had left behind, they gave us the names of leading dissidents remaining in Cuba. Through the good offices of the Swiss Embassy in Havana, we met eight of their designated conferees in the expectation they would confirm the entrenched opinion of the émigré leadership that neither the United States nor its citizens should have any dealings at all with Cuba, other than to enforce in whatever way possible a stringent embargo. Imagine our surprise when these "brave souls" told us that the best way to improve Cuba's governance was to "send a fleet of cruise ships" to her shores and dump our wacky, camera-lugging, fun-loving, irreverent tourists from one end of the island to the other. This, they said, would bring the regime to its knees in six months, unless, of course, it should close its ports to such unmonitored visitations despite the promise of dollar purchases, a decision hardly to be welcomed by the Cuban people.

Returning home, our group suggested to Congress that the United States lift restraints on travel and business. But the fact that the dog of our Cuba policy had been wagged by the tail of émigré sentiment for a generation meant that our unanimous report went into the permanent outbox without a whimper. It took another generation before President Obama would chart a new course for our relations with Cuba. *Ole!*

CAMP and CAVE

A year after I left Congress, Health, Education, and Welfare Secretary Joe Califano asked me to serve as executive director of one of his projects, FIPSE (the Fund for the Improvement of Post-Secondary Education). The purpose of this modest fund was to identify and support innovative approaches to education.

Among the grant recipients on my watch was CAMP (the College Assistance to Migrants Program), which provided tuition funds for children of migrant families on Texas farmlands who demonstrated learning potential at the high school level. It was a treat to attend the conferral of scholarships on these proud youngsters at the University of Texas in Austin.

Another program, entitled CAVE (the Committee to Avoid Violent Eruptions), was undertaken in Hampton Beach, New Hampshire, a quiet retirement community that had been overrun by teenagers with a propensity for mischief, including the harassment of old-timers along the boardwalk. The fund was used to erect a modest clubhouse at one end of the beach, which welcomed teenagers who would gain membership by signing a pledge to "behave." Such membership, signified by a button reading "CAVE," served notice to shopkeepers and patrons that the wearer came in peace to the shops and eateries along the boardwalk. Thus was written a happy chapter in the beach's book of experience.

"Not Another Word"

Several administrations later, my law partner, Fred Dombo, asked me to intercede on his behalf with Secretary of Defense Donald Rumsfeld, with whom I had served in Congress. My mission was to secure an appointment for Fred's client, Hoshyar Zebari, head of the Kurdish Democratic Party in Iraq. Don demurred but suggested I contact his deputy, Paul Wolfowitz, who agreed to see us. Mr. Zebari's intent was to alert our Defense Department that it would be a mistake to repose any confidence

Heard and Overheard

in his countryman Ahmed Chalabi (a leader of the anti-Saddam Iraqi National Congress), whom he described as a charlatan with no mandate to speak for Iraq. At this, Mr. Zebari was abruptly cut off by our indignant host, who said, "I will not hear another word against our good and loyal friend Ahmed Chalabi!" Visibly shaken, Mr. Zebari, clutching my arm, rose and departed.

In fairness to our host, his reaction reflected the current views of every relevant player in his chain of command, including presumably the Commander in Chief. However, Mr. Zebari's opinion seemed to be confirmed by subsequent events, including evidence of Mr. Chalabi's questionable ties with Iran.

United We Stand

Am I wrong in suggesting that congressional collegiality is preferable to confrontation? The public seems to think so and should have some say in the matter. Meanwhile the public understandably frets at the lemming-like tendency of its chosen representatives to dance on the precipices of domestic and foreign disaster, a worrisome prospect that is bad for the digestion. Bipartisanship per se is not irrefutable evidence of the decline of our Republic. It should in fact flourish in the most trying times.

That said, we should take comfort in the fact that today's Congress, despite its efforts to the contrary, is not the most contentious in history. Take, for example, the moment in 1856 when, on the floor of the Senate, Congressman Preston Brooks of South Carolina beat Senator Charles Sumner of Massachusetts senseless with his gold-headed cane, an act that was a symptomatic precursor, to be sure, of our Civil War. During my years in

Congress, we were more or less preoccupied with the Vietnam War, a divisive issue for certain, yet one that did not diminish mutual respect between members on both sides of the aisle. How to account for this?

For one thing, in those days we spent more time in each other's company both on the House floor and beyond it—thrown together, if you will, by the economics of our situation. In those days we were allotted only one trip home a month on Uncle Sam's nickel. Perforce we moved our families to Washington, and we socialized on weekends. Cross-aisle fraternization flourished on the job. I had no better friends in the House than Republican Leader Bob Michel of Illinois, Lou Frey of Florida, John Heinz of Pennsylvania, Bill Steiger of Wisconsin and Manuel Lujan of New Mexico.

As for Pete DuPont of Delaware, he and I cosponsored programs to bring high school students from our respective districts to Washington. We regularly stood in for each other, addressed each other's delegations, and committed impressionable students from our respective districts to each other's temporary care and instruction. Moreover, in those days there was a Congressional Wives caucus that brought the spouses of both parties together to share impressions and do good works in the D.C. area.

It may be that equivalent initiatives are undertaken today, but I cannot believe that being separated every weekend serves the cause of togetherness. A shining example of cross-aisle consideration was recently departed Speaker Tom Foley of the state of Washington. Testimonials to his collaborative brand of leadership shook the walls of the Capitol Rotunda at his memorial service on October 29, 2013, from President Obama, former

124   *Heard and Overheard*

President Bill Clinton, and his devoted wife, Heather. Senate Majority Leader Mitch McConnell and former House Minority Leader Bob Michel of Illinois brought the crowd of some three hundred to its feet with a heartfelt yet jolly remembrance of their joint years together in the people's house.

"I Don't Wear That Hat"

In my farewell address to Congress in 1977, I highlighted my last legislative proposal, the Youth Service Opportunity Act, in which I offered alternatives to a reconstituted military draft (as the latter was out of the question). The act gave qualified high school graduates the opportunity to enlist for one year in the military or for eighteen months in a non-military occupation relevant to emergency preparedness in the event of a natural calamity or war. These young people would be trained in disaster relief, triage treatment of the injured, firefighting, communications, transportation. Such certified service would entitle the volunteer to federal support for college tuition. My co-sponsor was Congressman Jonathan Bingham of New York. Preparedness was much on our minds when we coauthored this measure to assure readiness for different kinds of disasters that might involve physical damage. We believed if such a "balloon" were to go up, a ready reserve of trained young men and women who knew where to report and what to do would be of enormous benefit both to the outcome and to the participants. The bill did not get out of the Armed Services Committee, which deemed it an unwarranted infringement on its jurisdiction.

Shortly after 9/11/2001, a former colleague in Congress addressed a gathering of the U.S. Association of Former Members

Lyrics by Symington: an ad hoc quintet serenades President Johnson
aboard Air Force One in a photo signed by LBJ aide Liz Carpenter.

of Congress (FMC). Having served as chairman of the FMC, I asked the speaker, then the Secretary of Defense, if such training of our youngsters wouldn't be a good idea. "Yes," said Donald Rumsfeld, "but I don't wear that hat."

Next question: Who does? I wish I'd had the presence of mind to ask it.

"The Difference 'tween Dog and Man"

What brings the above caveat to mind is one of President Johnson's rueful reflections: "If you come upon a little puppy, injured on the road, and you pick him up, take him home, feed him, and nurse him back to health, why, don't cha know, that little pup will stand by you, comfort you, sustain you, and defend you, loyal and supportive to the very end! That's the difference 'tween a dog and a man."

PART TWO:
INNOCENCE ABROAD

In 1958, at the height of the Cold War, Jim visits Russia—and the
Church of the Savior on Spilled Blood in St. Petersburg.

LONDON

"Remarkable Fellow, Wasn't He?"

This was the appraisal by Britain's Prince Philip of legendary John Henry, the formidable railroad worker celebrated in song and story. It was by way of song that I had introduced the "steel drivin' man" to the guests gathered at the American Embassy for our ambassador's dinner for Queen Elizabeth II on March 12, 1958. Prince Philip proved to be an aficionado of American folk music and its variety of derivations from English, French, German, Spanish, and African sources. He saw it as confirmation of the melting pot phenomenon that defined our new world.

Our invitation to the dinner came by way of a telegram from Ambassador Whitney, my mother's first cousin. He wired us in St. Louis to fly over and join him in a dinner for "you know who." Sylvia and I assumed it was a birthday party for his stepdaughter, Kate Roosevelt Whitney. We assumed wrong. When the evening ended, Cousin Jock asked me to take a leave of absence from my St. Louis law firm and join his office as his special assistant, a position that provided total immersion in British-American relations.

"Out! Out!"

My first stay at the ambassador's official residence, Winfield House, antedated my assignment there as a very junior diplomat. Earlier, determined to end the Cold War armed with my guitar and rudimentary Russian language skills, I had planned a trip to Russia and booked a flight to Moscow with a layover in London. At the invitation of Cousins Jock and Betsey, I was billeted for the night in the mansion near Regents Park, despite their absence in the States for a holiday.

Arriving in the afternoon, I left that evening to call on my St. Bernard's schoolmate Azamat Guirey (who claimed to be a direct descendant of Genghis Khan) and his wife, Sylvia Obolensky, at their home in Eaton Square. With a wink, nod, and blown kiss to Sylvia, Azi whisked me off to a speakeasy called the Scheherazade. Whispering through a slot in the basement door, he secured our permission to enter. It was bedlam: a cacophony of balalaikas, guitars, and vodka-inspired toasts by a roomful of Russian émigrés—in short, my kind of party. I think I may have taken the stage at one point. In any event it was about 2 A.M. when, in an unsteady state, I was deposited back at Winfield House. Fumbling with the key providentially provided by the butler, Epps, I opened it—to sounds and sights, I think it fair to say, that I wouldn't have expected.

First the sounds: giggling and chortling from the adjacent living room; then the sights: a Rabelaisian orgy that might have met the demanding standards of the Marquis de Sade, to wit, five or six members of the all-male Embassy staff in undershorts or less, cavorting about the surprised furniture in a game of hide-and-seek with a number of similarly clad Bobbies (or Bobby pretenders), identifiable only by their distinctive hats.

Bleary of eye and aching of head, I was trying to decide what my role (if any) as a fleeting houseguest might be when the door from the foyer burst open, revealing the wrath of

Heard and Overheard

Jehovah in the imposing person of Epps. Resplendent in his bathrobe, with eyes blazing, he bellowed, "Out! Out!" The frightened occupants gathered their belongings in undignified haste and flitted through the French doors to the garden beyond.

I had taken the occasion to slip quietly up to my room and into the welcoming arms of Morpheus when a hard knock on the door catapulted me into a sitting position. It was Epps. Taking a seat by the bed, he said "I have failed. I shall be leaving the service." "No! No!" I cried. "The Whitneys need you now as never before." "You think so, sir?" "Absolutely!" "Very well then, we'll see," he sighed and departed, his bathrobe sash trailing on the floor.

Satisfied that I had put that chilling notion to rest, I settled once again for nature's balm. That is until a second sharp knock jolted me bolt upright. It was Cronin, the head footman. Baby-faced, with a distinctive shock of white hair, he had joined the Embassy staff after being relieved of similar duties in Buckingham Palace. "Sir," said Cronin, "John is crying." By "John" he referred to his assistant footman, who apparently feared retribution for his participation in the night's revelry. "He's in the kitchen. Will you come and reassure him?" Having no robe or slippers, I threw a raincoat over my pajamas and trudged, barefoot and doleful, behind Cronin as we made for the kitchen.

There indeed was John in tears. "You must think less of us," he moaned. "But, you know, we never have much fun. It was a chance to show our friends the upstairs rooms and the bathtub with gold taps." As the unappointed surrogate housemaster, I said, "Yes, John, but you must know how wrong it was of you to take advantage of your employers' absence, infringing on their personal privacy and, more importantly, the diplomatic status of this home." "Oh yes, yes," he sobbed, joined now by a chorus of "mmms" from the others. "Will you be telling on us?" "I shouldn't think so," I said, my head clearing. "You know it was wrong. It cannot be undone, but as far as I am concerned, it can go unmentioned. I've no doubt you will redouble your efforts to make this a secure and happy home for the Whitneys." "Indeed, sir!"

Not only did this prove to be the case, but their assiduous services over the next two years won both John and his accomplices permanent positions at Greentree, the Whitneys' Long Island home. Not until this writing have I ever mentioned what qualifies—albeit with a good deal of competition—as the most bizarre night of my life, one which would certainly have revved up the tabloids! Two years later I ran into Cronin in Washington's National Airport. He was on his way to assume the post of maître d' at the Dania Jai-Alai Palace in Hollywood, Florida.

"Use *Your* Judgment"

Although blissfully unaware of those events at his residence, Ambassador Whitney, after returning to his post, called me into his office to discuss my Scheherazade foray. "How did you know?" I asked. He replied, "MI5" (the British Security Service). Apparently one or more of their number made it a point to monitor evenings at the Scheherazade, which, although dedicated to the émigré community, were regularly attended by Soviet agents. My next foolish question: "Should I not return?" was answered cheerfully, "Why not use *your* judgment?"

"Stone Walls Do Not a Prison Make"

Among the guests at the Whitneys' 1959 dinner for Princess Margaret was her Lady-in-Waiting, Elizabeth Cavendish. A kindly spinster, Lady Elizabeth served in a volunteer capacity as Director of Visits to Prisons, including Wandsworth, a high-security facility for multiple offenders and men convicted of capital crimes. Following dinner, at the Ambassador's suggestion, I brought out my guitar and sang some folk songs.

As goodnights were said, Lady Elizabeth drew me aside and asked whether I might be persuaded to sing for "her" prisoners. A week later I found myself standing before one of the most ominous structures in Christendom. Escorted by Lady Elizabeth and two armed guards, I entered through the backstage door of a gloomy auditorium populated by rows of frowning prisoners in dark suits. The raised four corners of the high-ceilinged room featured sentries with submachine guns at the ready; not your usual venue. Lady Elizabeth had taken a seat directly behind me and next to the warden, when the latter unaccountably excused himself and departed. To relieve the ensuing silence, I said, "Not to worry, he'll be right back; he's a trusty." Hearty laughter dispelled the gloom. Sensing an aversion to the sad or sentimental, I stayed with such cheery nonsense as "Old Dan Tucker" and "Ragtime Cowboy Joe."

Escorted by local dignitaries, Ambassador Whitney prepares to visit
British industrial sites with his special assistant in his wake.

Opening the floor to questions, I was startled by the first one: "What do you think of Monty's book?" In his newly published autobiography, Field Marshal Bernard Montgomery had assigned a major portion of the credit for victory over Germany to his own good self—with Eisenhower playing a supporting role. Although I had just finished reading this engaging work, I thought it the better part of discretion to say I looked forward to it. By then the warden had returned to thank us and escort us to the prison gate. As it clanged behind us, it occurred to me that the Cavalier poet Richard Lovelace, who wrote "Stone walls do not a prison make, nor iron bars a cage," had yet to visit Wandsworth.

"Correspondence between Nonagenarians"

"There's an old fellow out here who wants to see the Ambassador," said the receptionist at our embassy in London one summer afternoon in 1958. "Says he has a question for him." Ambassador Whitney was on home leave, so I as his assistant stepped into the waiting room. There, holding a crumpled felt hat, stood a stooped, white-bearded ancient. His once elegant tweed suit was now short of buttons and long on soup stains and cigarette burns.

"I am Baron Meyendorff," he said, "and I've come here to inquire into the health of Senator Green. I read in a magazine that he was not well."

Senator Theodore F. Green of Rhode Island, at ninety years of age, was then the oldest member of Congress. I asked the Baron how they became acquainted. "We were in school together in

Austria," he replied, "in the 1890s. You can reach me at the Refugee Home on Cromwell Street. Good day."

I wrote the Senator at once, telling him of the visit of a gentleman I could best describe as a "Santa Claus fallen on hard times." Within a week I received a letter from the Senator informing me that Baron Alexander von Meyendorff was the most distinguished living Russian and, moreover, a friend of his youth. Folded in the letter was a $200 check that the Senator warned me not to give to the Baron, as he would immediately make it over to someone he considered less fortunate. "Find out what he needs," the Senator wrote, "and get it for him."

I began the mission by calling on Miss Agnew, the austere British lady who ran the Refugee Home. Commenting on the respect shown him by his fellow East European castaways, she recalled the earlier visit of a lady aristocrat of old Russia, who said they had danced together in the czar's palace at the turn of the century. Learning of the Baron's whereabouts, she had come to pay him a visit. Advised that this grande dame was waiting downstairs, he said, "Send her away. She's a pest." Addressing my mission, Miss Agnew continued, "he needs pajamas and a bathrobe, yes, and a shirt, ascot tie, and, oh yes, a new chair."

Having met all those requirements at Harrods, I phoned to say I would be calling on the Baron at teatime. Meeting me at the door, he led me into the sitting room, where an assortment of his contemporaries were playing cards. "Out," he said in a voice that was accustomed to command. They departed like wraiths into the hallway, leaving the two of us sitting by the window in the late afternoon sunlight.

"Now," he said, sitting back, "why have you come?" Hesitant

Heard and Overheard

to broach the subject, I began by reporting that I had notified Senator Green of his visit to the Embassy and the reason for it. "Fine, fine," said the Baron.

"And the Senator was delighted to hear of you."

"Yes, yes, that's fine."

"And he wanted to be remembered to you."

"Oh, well, yes, that's nice," said the Baron.

"In that connection," I said, "he wished me to express his pleasure in hearing from you by providing some things you might need."

The Baron, getting the point and noting my discomfort, said, "Don't be embarrassed, young man. I've been in your position many times."

This was my cue to present him with the shirt and tie. "Ridiculous," he muttered, donning the latter with a deft twirl.

"That's not all," I said.

"Oh dear! Well, would you like to see my room?"

"Certainly."

We climbed the rickety stairs to a third-floor bedroom. No more than ten feet square, it contained an unmade bed, a chest, and an armchair that sank to the floor. The new one had not arrived. He then told me about his life. His mother, he said, was a lover of Franz Liszt. His family had owned enormous estates in pre-revolutionary Russia. A historian by profession, he was the technical advisor for Bernard Pares' exhaustive *A History of Russia*. He told me his wife had died a few years earlier, and was buried in the coastal town of Torquay.

"If the Senator wishes to help me further," he said, "I should like to be buried next to my wife."

He also told me he would write to thank Senator Green. "But you know," he reflected, "correspondence between nonagenarians is a difficult thing." When I asked him how he spent his time, he said he walked every day to the library of the British Museum, a mile up the road.

"Surely you could take a bus," I suggested. "No, indeed," he replied. "I'm afraid I'd pop off and be a bother to the driver."

When I returned to the States to join my father's presidential campaign, I received a letter from Miss Agnew relating that the Baron had passed on, and was buried as he wished.

"Sing!"

Every one of our diplomatic missions is expected to provide effusive hospitality to visiting Congressmen—from whence cometh their funding. The Court of St. James's was no exception. In 1959 John Rooney, the feisty bantam-sized chairman of the relevant House Appropriations subcommittee, was about to descend on our London Embassy with an eye to trimming its budget. His mission sent chills all down the line. Arriving on a government plane with his party of cost cutters, Rooney, short of stature (and of temper when crossed) was driven to the Connaught Hotel for a night's rest before reviewing our operations.

As Ambassador Whitney was traveling at home, he invited our Deputy Chief of Mission Walworth (Wally) Barbour, and a few others on staff to an arrival dinner at the Connaught. Having heard that I'd sung on BBC, he suggested I serenade the group. When he gave the nod I stood up and sang "Danny Boy" for them and other bemused diners. Over coffee the chairman suggested we adjourn to his suite, where he would like to hear more songs. These I provided until his whiskey-dimmed eyes fluttered into sleep. The next morning we were advised that he had phoned to say he considered everything shipshape in our operation and was headed on to Paris. And lo, I was a hero among the Hittites.

A decade later, on entering the House chamber as a new member, I encountered the Chairman, who looked at me blankly for a second and then growled with a grin, "Sing!"

"The Living Will Envy the Dead"

Later that year we assembled in the Ambassador's private dining room for a dinner in honor of Averell Harriman, former governor of New York and ambassador to both Great Britain and the Soviet Union. The subject discussed was the increasingly strained relations between Russia and China, which had even featured a border skirmish along the Ussuri River. Harriman took the occasion to recount conversations with the leaders of the two countries during his recent travels. The first meeting produced Chairman Mao's serene reaction to Russia's nuclear threat: "Yes, they could kill 300 million of us, but there would be 300 million left." According to Harriman, when he conveyed this to Premier Khrushchev, the latter responded, "Yes, and the living will envy the dead."

"Don't Be Deceived"

"Don't be deceived! The alliance between China and Russia is solid and durable."

"Don't be deceived! Russia and China will always be at swords' points."

Governor Harriman made both of these utterances in my presence, the first at the Embassy dinner in his honor. When I had raised reports of an apparent fraying of Sino-Soviet relations, the Governor emphatically rejected the notion, "Don't be deceived," he said.

Some twenty years later, during dinner at his Virginia estate, I called attention to a report that differences which had arisen in the interim were in the process of being reconciled. "Nonsense," said Harriman. "Russia and China are natural antagonists and will remain so."

Who was it said "a foolish consistency is the hobgoblin of small minds"? Governor Harriman was anything but small-minded.

Nixon and the Three Bs

In 1959 Vice President Nixon flew to England to dedicate a memorial in St. Paul's Cathedral to American airmen killed in action over Europe. Hosting the Embassy's dinner for the Queen, he learned that Sylvia had played piano for Her Majesty at a previous reception. Taking us both aside after dinner, he confided in hushed tones, "I used to know everything there was to know about Bach, Beethoven, and Brahms."

"How Very Diplomatic"

The stately mansion Winfield House, the ambassador's London residence, was also the site of a dinner in honor of the

Queen's younger sister, Princess Margaret, shortly after I arrived in 1959. As the Princess brought along her little Pekinese dog, Cousin Jock was moved to observe, "From Nationalist China, I presume." "No," answered the Princess, "*Proper* China!" Britain, unlike the United States at the time, recognized the communist government on the mainland. There was a brief but embarrassing silence, which I broke, saying, "In any event, China proper." "How very diplomatic!" exclaimed the Princess. Weeks later at the Queen's annual diplomatic reception for all embassies at Windsor Castle, I stood in the back row of our delegation, being junior in rank. As the Queen and Princess walked slowly by, shaking hands with each Chief of Mission, the Princess pushed her way through to shake mine. "What did you do wrong?" quipped one of my colleagues.

"I Could Not Have Won the War"

Among my extracurricular assignments in London was the forging of Field Marshal Bernard Montgomery's signature on his autobiography. As commander of British forces in their 1942 victory at El Alamein over Germany's vaunted Afrika Korps under the command of the "Desert Fox," Field Marshal Erwin Rommel, he had earned a secure place in the annals of British military history. The subsequent battle for total victory in Europe brought him under the direction of Allied Supreme Commander Dwight Eisenhower.

Smaller in physical stature than in self-esteem, "Monty" tried the patience of our beloved Ike to a point that was apparent to his entire command, including Ira Eaker, Commander of the U.S. Eighth Air Force. As Eaker's good friend and former subaltern in his intelligence service, Jock Whitney hit upon the idea of having Monty inscribe his book to him. Since that was unlikely, he assigned me the task. After a few tries, I produced a credible version of Jock's text, which I affixed to the frontispiece: "To Ira Eaker, without whose loyal support I could not have won the war—(signed) Montgomery of Alamein." The book, in official wrappings covered with royal stamps, seemed to warrant immediate delivery. Accordingly, it was rushed to the golf course where Eaker was measuring his putt on the eighteenth green. Observers reported that he tore it open, gazed in disbelief, and then burst out laughing.

"It's Kirk Douglas!"

I was standing beside the ambassador while he bade farewell to the hundreds of American citizens who had attended the 4th of July reception at Winfield House. The mansion was festooned with works of art from his own private collection. Among them: Renoir's *The Ball at the Moulin de la Galette,* Picasso's *Boy with a Pipe,* Thomas Eakins' *The Oarsmen,* and, centered in the dining room, glaring at the viewer, the haunting Van Gogh self-portrait that had been on the cover of a best-selling biography, *Lust for Life,* which in turn became a hit movie. This evoked a cry of delight from one of the guests. "Look!" he enthused. "It's Kirk Douglas!" As the star-struck visitors departed, another, taking his host's hand in both of his, gushed, "Mr. Ambassador, I didn't know you paint!"

"Tired of Sin? Step In!"

This welcoming message graced the entrance of a little church in East London that I noticed in 1959. Beneath it someone had penciled, "If not, call Chelsea 7-2405."

RUSSIA

"These People Aren't Going to Quit"

My quest for a more durable relationship with Russia was initially sparked by my grandfather, Congressman James W. Wadsworth Jr. of New York. A veteran of the Spanish-American War, he had chaired the Military Affairs Committee of the Senate in World War I and was elected to the House in 1932, six years after failing to secure a third term in the Senate. An influential legislator in both wars, he was drawn to the qualities of endurance that marked the Russian nature.

I was fourteen in the summer of 1942 when, between radio reports by Lowell Thomas about the siege of Stalingrad, Granddad would play Russian liturgical music on the Victrola. Over the booming basses and soaring tenors, he turned to me and said, "These people aren't going to quit." I decided then to get to know "these people."

Six years later during the Berlin Airlift, my father, then Secretary of the Air Force, suggested that my brother and I "get to know Russia. You'll be fightin' 'em or doing business with 'em in your lifetime." He made this sobering assessment following our discharges from the Army and Marines, respectively, in 1946, when Dad's orientation was shaped by the nerve-racking postwar initiatives of Marshal Stalin. Tim and I then headed off to Yale, where Tim signed up for a Russian course, which rendered him fluent in a couple of years. Being more interested in French and Spanish, I dawdled until the Korean War broke out and lines were drawn that seemed to confirm my father's grim augury. During my first year of law practice in St. Louis, I sought and luckily found two marvelous teachers of the subject, Mrs. Danett and Madame Gogotsky. The former taught at my old school, St. Louis Country Day, the latter at Berlitz. Between them, they brought me up to the threshold of competence.

My growing curiosity about "these people"—their capacity to endure and their stream of genius in music, literature and the lively arts—led to a trip in July 1958 to Leningrad, Kiev, and Moscow. Guitar in hand, armed with folk songs of both countries, and equipped with a rudimentary command of the language, I met scores of Russian citizens in the parks and squares of those cities. Despite strategically placed loud speakers denouncing "Americanski aggression" (in Lebanon), the people were uniformly welcoming and, needless to say, curious. How many man-hours did it take to buy my shoes, shirt, and sweater? Did American wives all do hard work? How many families lived in one apartment? Did one need a passport to go to Chicago from New York? Could you go to church? Would you lose your job if you went to church? Will you write to us? But only from inside Russia, please, not from abroad.

These sad inquires would be interspersed with such proud if questionable assertions as "We out-produce you in wheat, beef, and eggs!"

The successful launch into orbit of little Laika, a stray dog garbed in cosmonaut attire, generated the only self-criticism I encountered in Russia. "Such cruelty to a helpless animal should not be permitted," said an elderly lady out of earshot of the plainclothes police who normally monitored our conversations.

Somehow I managed to be forthright without incurring

Had guitar, did travel: Jim makes merry with newfound Russian friends during his private good will tour in 1958.

official displeasure, despite the inevitable silent participants in these gatherings. One old fellow summed things up this way: "As I understand it," he said, "in America you can do pretty much as you please as long as you don't hurt anyone else." Another time I was standing with a group in the street examining a rare American car (a Ford). An official approached us and told me in English to move off the street. When I hastened to do so, several onlookers asked what he had said, and I told them. "We stay," they said. "It is our street." A fine point that I doubt would have carried in their contemporary courts of law. But the impulse to be governed justly was obstinate.

"America Wants War?"

This was the question frequently put to me by hopeful yet skeptical Russians. My trip had occurred at an awkward moment. A force of U.S. Marines had only recently landed in Lebanon to shore up the regime of President Camille Chamoun, a presumably trustworthy Christian leader threatened by a communist takeover. A British force had entered Jordan on a similar mission to provide support to young King Hussein. Accordingly, loudspeakers strategically located at street intersections were unsparing in their denunciation of *"Amerikanski and Angliski aggression."*

It was no surprise then to be so accosted in painful tones by a citizenry still reeling from their sacrifices in the Great Patriotic War. My answer, *"Nyet! Amerika nyeh khochet voynoo!"* (No! America does not want war) was sufficiently reassuring to set the stage for another shared evening of folk songs in the park.

150   *Heard and Overheard*

"Who Are These People?"

American visitors to Russia were in short supply in the late 1950s, and objects of friendly curiosity. Emerging with hundreds of fellow tourists from St. Petersburg's gilded Hermitage Museum, I found myself surrounded by a dozen inquiring citizens of swarthier complexion than the rest. I asked them what part of Russia they were from. "Tashkent!" was their proud response. At this point, our Intourist guide, a plump little lady who had herded us through the palace, pulled me aside and asked, "Who are these people?" "Your fellow citizens," I replied. "Not at all," she scoffed. "They must be from some Asian country." Subsequent events have indeed restored their own nationality to such "outsiders."

"Your Visa Has Expired"

This was the curt advisory given me over the phone in my room in the Hotel Moskva. What had apparently occasioned the call was my earlier request to the Russian Intourist agent to be put in touch with one Armand Hammer, namesake of his famous uncle and the son of his brother Victor. Decades earlier, Lenin's "New Economic Policy" had tolerated foreign business for a brief period, and the brothers Hammer had prospered in several enterprises, perhaps the least of which involved shipping Russian art objects and precious artifacts to a gallery they operated on New York's 57th Street. When the policy was changed and expropriation threatened, the Hammers removed all their treasures—and themselves—to New York. Victor's Russian wife, however, declined to accompany him to America and remained in Russia with an infant son he had never seen.

My mission, assigned by my cousin Kate Roosevelt (granddaughter of FDR), was to find, on behalf of her friend Victor, this long-lost son and present him with a few gifts. One of these was a supply of insulin for his mother, Victor's long-estranged wife who, he learned, had developed diabetes. Apparently my attempt to contact a Russian citizen was considered inappropriate by the authorities, and the phone call was made, presumably to dissuade me from pursuing the matter. I was sufficiently irked to lodge a complaint at the Intourist desk in the lobby. By a stroke of fortune, the agent I picked turned out to have been Cousin Kate's escort on a previous occasion.

"My name is Igor," he said, "but you can call me Harry." "Okay, Harry, what next?" "I will find this man," he promised.

I heard nothing more from "Harry" until the eve of our departure, when he suddenly called. "I have your man," he said. "Really? Put him on." After a moment a deep voice said, "Hello." "Armand Hammer?" I asked. "Yes." "I have a message from your father. Can you come here?" "Yes."

I answered the knock on the door to find a handsome lookalike of a young Orson Welles. He seemed transfixed by the sight of a group of my new young friends gathered around the piano the hotel had provided in the room. Bidding goodnight to them all, I led young Armand into an adjoining room and presented his Dad's gifts of shirts, ties, a fountain pen, and finally the insulin. At that point he burst into tears. *"Ochen vazhni,"* he said. (Very important.)

I asked him why he didn't come to the States for a visit. It was because, he said, his wife would not be allowed to accompany him—a Soviet precaution to discourage defection.

Heard and Overheard

"Where's the Soap?"

The suite assigned me at the Hotel Moskva was furnished with sofas, chairs, artwork, tables, and the grand piano. However, there was no soap in the bathroom. Hence my anguished outcry to no one in particular in the empty room: "Where's the soap?"

Returning from dinner that evening I found an abundance of soap in and around the bath. It occurred to me that we couldn't get that kind of service in America—nor want it!

Are We *Not* Being Watched?

In 1958 I came across a *London Times* report of a Soviet training center designed to acquaint students of espionage with the customs and mores of Americans. This fetching idea prompted me to compose *Schenectograd*, a musical featuring a patriotic young graduate, Avrahm Spunktov, whose assignment is to come to the United States and find unemployment. Regrettably—from his standpoint—he is hugely popular, cannot avoid employment, and marries the boss's daughter, all the while reassuring his Soviet principals that corruption in America is so pervasive that he simply needs more time to explore its contours.

Recent disclosures of the surveillance society we may have become (via the good offices of the National Security Agency), suggest that truth is once again well on its way to trump fiction. Perish the thought that an American might one day say "I have the uneasy feeling that we are not being watched."

"We Would Rather Have Technology"

Retiring from Congress in 1977, I joined former Senator George Smathers of Florida and his Miami-based partner, Sydney Herlong, to form the law firm Smathers, Symington and Herlong. A beloved client of the firm was the Bourbon Institute, a noble venture whose object in life was to promote the consumption of this heartwarming beverage. Believing it had never been introduced to Russia and determined to correct this oversight, I secured an appointment with Ambassador Dobrynin. As I settled in the easy chair he offered, I found myself face-to-face with a silver tray bearing two shot glasses of Stolichnaya. This presented the opening to cut to the chase of my visit. Pointing out America's long affair with Russia's national drink, I suggested it was time for reciprocal hospitality to be extended to ours. The Ambassador paused a moment before replying, "We would rather have technology."

"Is Like Foreign Minister"

On a summer evening in 1967, I was untimely ripped from a pleasant al fresco dinner among friends by a White House phone call with instructions to get to Andrews Air Force Base within an hour. Apparently, at the conclusion of the Glassboro Talks, President Lyndon B. Johnson had offered to fly his guest, Premier Alexei Kosygin, to any spot in the United States that he might wish to visit. Niagara Falls was chosen, and I was directed to meet and escort the Premier and his party aboard Air Force Two for the trip. Arriving at Andrews, I boarded the plane to check the interior, just in time to hide some racy magazines strewn throughout.

Heard and Overheard

Minutes later a long line of black limousines drew up to the ramp, and out stepped Kosygin, Foreign Minister Andrei Gromyko, Ambassador Dobrynin, and some thirty members of their party.

After a smooth short flight, we landed at an airport serving the falls and were met by the Mayor, who had the intriguing name of E. Dent Lackey. On the limo ride to the site of the falls, Kosygin asked the Mayor what he did for a living besides his mayoral duties. Lackey proudly described himself as a "public relations man." Genuinely puzzled, Kosygin asked, "What is public relations man?" Before Lackey could assemble his thoughts, Gromyko, with no change of expression, mused, "Is like Foreign Minister."

"Everything with Cross and Gun"

Accepting an invitation to visit the Canadian side of the falls, Kosygin, Gromyko, and Dobrynin were conducted to a reception area that featured an enormous mural depicting a troop of seventeenth-century French soldiers with helmets and breast-plates, cautiously making their way through an Indian-infested wilderness, muskets at the ready. Their leader was holding high a giant wooden cross. Kosygin stopped at the site, gazed upward, and muttered, "Everything with cross and gun!" A true non-believer.

"You Want Players from Evil Empire!"

In the 1980s it was a matter of common knowledge that Russia produced first-class hockey players. They were so good, in fact, that our National Hockey League teams sought their services, even those who were deemed "graybeards"—players over twenty-five and presumably past their prime. As such, an arrangement would have to be made with the Soviet government. Bob Ziegler, owner of the New Jersey Devils, and National Hockey League President John Whitehead asked my assistance in presenting their case to Ambassador Dobrynin. I called and secured an appointment for the three of us. This was shortly after President Reagan's famous characterization of the "evil empire." Thus, after our clients had stated their case, Dobrynin leaned back and laughed, "I get it; you want players from Evil Empire to play with Devils!"

Score one for the empire! The resulting arrangements led to an infusion of Russian hockey players in the league who have won the hearts of fans all over, including Washington, D.C., where they are currently treated to the mastery of Alex Ovechkin and his Russian teammates.

"Why Not Down Here?"

In 1972, as chairman of the House Subcommittee on Science and Technology, I held hearings on the so-called Moscow Accords, by which President Nixon and Premier Brezhnev had agreed to share information in the fields of health (including alcoholism), science, and space. The latter resulted in the historic Apollo–Soyuz Test Project, in which the two spacecraft were carefully maneuvered to permit docking and the exchange of occupants. The designer of the docking module (and subsequently of the *Mir*–Shuttle link-up) was Russia's Vladimir Syromyatnikov. A jolly genius with a delightful sense

Heard and Overheard

of humor, he was my guest at Washington's Metropolitan Club where, over "a cup of kindness" (vodka), we decided that the successful "embrace in space" should be a lesson to our respective political authorities. If we could get along up there, why not down here?

President Lincoln and Czar Alexander II

My return to private life and law enabled me, through the medium of the American-Russian Cultural Cooperation Foundation (ARCCF), to set the course of the final leg of my journey toward the "promised land," a steady state of comity between our two nations. In the words of Walt Whitman, in his preface to a proposed Russian translation of *Leaves of Grass*, we are "so different yet so alike. . . . As my dearest dream is for an internationality of poems and poets, binding the lands of earth closer than all treaties and diplomacy. . . . How happy I should be to get the hearing and emotional contact of the great Russian peoples."

A few years ago, with the planning of the Lincoln Bicentennial in its infant state, it occurred to me that Lincoln's friendly correspondence with Czar Alexander II was a page missing from our textbooks. Yet more has been lost than history itself. Absent from media attention is the contemporary relevance of that history. Relevance and resonance relating not only to the parallel initiatives of the two leaders to strike the chains of bondage and set their respective courses to more just societies, but to the Czar's manifesto establishing independent courts and juries, together with his plan at the time of his death to broaden those freedoms. These aspirations were scotched by his aggrieved and angry son, Czar Alexander III, whose crackdown aborted his father's dream, shackled his bewildered successor, Nicholas II, and, with the help of World War I, opened a return to totalitarianism with a new face. Yet now, by a strike of chronological fortune, our two countries and peoples could not only bask in the glow of this remembered partnership but be inspired by it to renew our respective commitments to the causes for which Lincoln and Alexander lived and died.

With the thought that poets often have a better take on life than politicians, I arranged with the Russian Peace Commission and Russian sculptor Alexander Bourganov to erect a noble statue of Whitman at the entrance to Moscow University. Unveiled by Secretary of State Hillary Clinton and Russian Foreign Minister Sergei Lavrov, it sends its message of hope across the campus and out into the country. We then prevailed on Mr. Bourganov to craft an imposing statue of Russia's immortal poet Alexander Pushkin on the campus of George Washington University. Inscribed on its pedestal: "With my lyre I have called for peace and an end to human suffering."

During the ARCCF's year-long "President Lincoln and Alexander II" celebration of the joint lives and achievements of the two leaders, Russia's Ambassador to the United States, Sergei Kislyak, accepted our invitation to address a Kansas City gathering on Lincoln's 200th birthday, February 12, 2009. With excellent English and a cheerful manner, he dwelt on the similarities of challenge the two leaders confronted, the cordial relations they enjoyed, and their joint imprint on history. In this connection I quote an exchange of dispatches between Bayard Taylor,

Heard and Overheard

our Chargé d'Affaires in St. Petersburg, and Secretary of State William Seward.

Dispatch of the U.S. Chargé d'Affaires in St. Petersburg, Bayard Taylor, to Secretary of State William H. Seward on the Judicial Reform issued by Alexander II, October 25, 1862:

Sir: I have the honor to report to you the promulgation of His Imperial Majesty which is universally pronounced to be second in importance in its effect upon the future of Russia only to that of the emancipation of the serfs. It is no less than a plan or basis for the thorough reorganization of the administration of justice throughout the empire, whereby the innumerable abuses, possible under the prevailing system, are prevented, and the great body of the people receive, in addition to personal liberty, an equal protection in the enjoyment of their individual rights.

Dispatch of Secretary of State William H. Seward to Bayard Taylor, U.S. Chargé d'Affaires, November 24, 1862:

The decree of the Emperor which establishes an independent and impartial judiciary ... is calculated to command the approval of mankind. It seems to secure to Russia the benefits without the calamities of revolution.... Constitutional nations which heretofore have regarded the friendship between Russia and the United States as wanting a foundation in common principles and sentiments, must hereafter admit that this relation is as natural in its character as it is auspicious to both countries in its result.

In my view the "natural" aspect of the "relation" should survive every transitory test.

FOOD FOR PEACE

"You Gringo Protestant"

Title 3 of Public Law 480 (the legislation that established the Food For Peace program) provided for gifts of grain, powdered milk, and other surplus commodities to the world's hungry through such charitable entities as CARE, Caritas (Catholic Relief), and Church World Service.

A month after President Kennedy's inauguration, as deputy director of the program led by George McGovern, I found myself in Leticia, overlooking the dust-covered rooftops of Lima, Peru. We inaugurated a school lunch program for the thousand youngsters living there in caves and cardboard-covered shacks, with no dependable source of food and a reliance for water on puddles that formed at the base of the hill. With the volunteer participation of fathers and mothers, a new school refectory was to be built and staffed to serve one nourishing meal a day. It would consist of U.S.-donated bulgur wheat (which can be cooked like rice) and powdered milk reconstituted with water from a reliable source, plus vegetables grown in home gardens.

In August of that year I returned to view the results. The children were all smiles, as were their parents. A leading spokesman for the latter asked me if I would consent to serve as *padrino* or godfather to the children as the parents exchanged their marriage vows. "Surely," I replied, "the parents are married!" "No, indeed!" I was then told that a marriage ceremony cost something in the nature of five dollars as compensation to the church. This seemed an unnecessary burden to parents whose children might not live out their childhood. But now that they could eat and live, they should have *dignidad*.

A proud moment it was to stand beside some one hundred couples as each in turn was sprinkled with holy water, to the delight of their smiling children. At the conclusion of the ceremony, the old priest turned to me and said, "I have been trying to marry these good people for years—and you gringo Protestant got it done in a summer."

"We Should Do Nothing to Reduce the Death Rate"

In October 1962 I attended the United Nations Food and Agricultural Organization's epic conference in Rome. Most of the speakers dwelt on statistics, tonnages, shipping strategies, and controls. That is until the Brazilian delegate named Castro (no relation to Fidel) rose to question the rationale for providing food at little or no cost to needy nations, saying, "We should do nothing to reduce the death rate in the third world." He based his conclusion on his calculation that the world's population would soon outrun its food supply. As merely an observer at the conference, I was hesitant to speak up. But I thought I had to put a marker on this argument. So I raised my hand and, when recognized, stated that President Kennedy did not run for office on a pledge to maintain the death rate in any part of the world.

But the Malthusian theory of population outpacing the world's food supply does not go gently into the night. I'm reminded of a suggestion made on the House floor by my fellow Congressman from Missouri, Jerry Litton. During a 1976 discussion of foreign aid, he proposed to deny food assistance to nations that did not institute acceptable population controls. His reasoning echoed that of University of Pennsylvania Professor

Loren Eiseley, who had floated the notion that man was a spore consuming its host, Earth, and that our space program represented a dawning recognition of the need to look for a new home. Jerry and I were matched that fall in the Senate primary, which he won handily before being tragically killed in a plane crash the night of his victory.

The inescapable logic of numbers buttresses the case for population control. The question is whether to achieve this result by limiting the food supply, with its consequences of disease and starvation, or through the voluntary undertaking by parents to have fewer children. The latter option runs counter to the strictures of the Catholic Church, whose influence in this respect prevails in many areas of the world, China being a significant exception. In that country the restriction to one or two children per family is, sadly, not an option but a requirement.

"Tenemos un Yanqui!"

President Kennedy's visionary program, the "Alliance for Progress" was launched at a 1961 inter-American Conference on the Americas in Punta del Este, Uruguay, but Cuba's incendiary disciple Che Guevara took center stage. Serious economists like Brazil's brilliant young Celso Furtado pressed in to catch Guevara's every word. It was Che's day, and a star-struck crowd surrounded him throughout the proceedings. The following night we were all invited to a black-tie reception in the local museum. Striking paintings by Uruguayan artists lined the walls of the old building. Cocktails were served and commemorative medals distributed by the proud Mayor to all the delegates. I noticed three shabbily dressed young men standing in a corner. Long-haired and open-shirted, they looked sullenly out on the crowd. I asked them which delegation they represented. "We are from the world of painters," said their spokesman.

"You mean you have done some of these works?" I asked. "Of course." "But where are the others?" "We are chosen to represent them all."

I told them I would like to meet their friends and fellow artists. "You mean you would leave this place?" *"Certeza."* (Sure.)

We soon piled into a 1940 Ford with exposed engine, chuffing along a dirt road into the woods. Ten minutes later we pulled up at a beautiful tree-shaded home, which we entered to find some thirty young men and women seated on its spacious living room floor. They were being regaled by a bearded young fire-eater. His subject: *el imperialismo yanqui.* Interrupting his monologue, my escort shouted proudly, *"Tenemos un yanqui!"* (We got a Yankee!) The group fell silent. *"Explica,"* someone said.

I recalled an expression that reflected the importance of the guitar to Spanish culture. If one were to speak eloquently one spoke *"con* [with] *guitar;"* if clumsily, *"sin* [without] *guitar."* *"No puedo explicarme sin guitar,"* I said. As I might have expected, and fervently hoped, a guitar was immediately produced. After a couple of ballads, *"Fulgida Luna"* (Full Moon) and *"El Céfiro"* (The Zephyr), we engaged in a lengthy exchange of hopes and ideas, ending only when the hostess, Elsie Rivero Haedo, tall and beautiful, entered the room. After bidding farewell to her young guests, she told me I had done something

Heard and Overheard

President Kennedy chose George McGovern to lead Food For Peace,
his international initiative, with Jim Symington as his deputy director.

"muy importante," putting a "human face" on the colossus of the North. She explained her hospitality to the restless young visitors as giving them a "safe house" to vent their emotions without getting arrested.

"Don't Say We Asked"

In 1961 China was experiencing a severe shortfall in harvests that occasioned its offer to buy a half billion dollars' worth of wheat from the United States or any other source. George McGovern, director of Food For Peace, sent me to the headquarters of the National Farmers Organization (NFO) in Seattle to discuss the request. The NFO and its President, the well-known agriculturalist Clifford Hope, were strongly Republican and definitely reluctant to be seen "doing business with the devil." I was first advised that they might approve the sale, with the caveat, "Don't say we asked." Nevertheless, hardliners opposed the idea of doing business with godless communists, and they prevailed. Canada, unhampered by such purist reservations, got the business and made the money, a fair sum in those days.

A similar conflict of interest surfaced March 15, 2012, in the Senate Finance Committee as Republican members opposed the long-overdue initiative to remove from the books the anachronistic Jackson-Vanik amendment, which had been put in place in 1971 as a response to Russia's policy of denying its Jewish citizens the right to emigrate. The policy, long since relegated to the scrapheap of history, has continued to serve as a handy vehicle in dealing with an unrelated series of grievances. Credit for the overdue removal of Jackson-Vanik from our statute books must go to my former House colleague, Senate Finance Chairman Max Baucus, whose trip to Russia in March 2012 convinced him of the commonsense need to leave that law to another age.

"Where Can I Take a Trolley?"

At a farewell dinner in Buenos Aires, the last stop on my 1961 Food For Peace tour of South America, I was asked where and how I had studied Spanish. "Yale," I said, and described Señor Gaona, my Mexican-American professor, who required memorization of *fraces* (phrases) to make us more familiar with everyday speech. *"Un ejemplo* [an example]!" they demanded. Searching my mind for apt contenders, I came up with an unfortunate choice: *"Donde puede coger un tranvía?"*—which I confidently believed to express "Where can I take a trolley?" The burst of hilarity this produced was explained by the fact that the word *"coger"* in Argentina means to take not a trolley, but a woman.

"Capitalist Nag"

In his engaging treatise, *For Victory in the Peaceful Competition with Capitalism,* Soviet Premier Nikita Khrushchev claimed the "capitalist nag" would never "drag its chariot to victory over the Communist horse." Perhaps he had forgotten the old Russian proverb, "It is not the horse that pulls the cart; it's the grain." He had the proverb. We had the grain.

The Food For Peace programs involved with urban schools were easier to service due to their proximity to supplies. Less fortunate were the youngsters of the more remote areas. Nevertheless, in the village of Puno in the high plains of Peru, I joined with Undersecretary of State Chester Bowles in 1961 to inaugurate a school lunch program for thirty thousand youngsters. To Sylvia I penned an irreverent account of the consequent celebration as follows:

This place is 13,000 feet up. Everyone is fainting except the Indians. And they weren't paying much attention either. They wear little bowler hats, and red capes. Their faces look cut from brown clay with about as much expression as you might expect from a fellow whose civilization was interrupted four centuries back. But then they got out their reed pipes and knocked out a little pentatonic ditty as I strummed feebly on my guitar, gasping for air. They were drinking chicha, a fermented corn beverage. With that, who needs air? All you need is a place to lie down. And there's lots of room for that. Ground, they've got. But you couldn't raise a cactus on it. It's rock hard—covered with a green furze you couldn't dignify with the name grass. You couldn't scrape it off with a pen knife. The cattle are a bony bunch, either lying down or grazing knee deep in the waters of icy Lake Titicaca on weeds—and maybe a few slow fish, for all I know. Anyway, the kids are going to eat for a change. And this might start something.

I opened the program with a carefully crafted five-minute speech. I hoped to make points by giving it in Spanish, forgetting that they didn't speak it. But it was translated into Aymara and/or Quechua by a fiery little lady who spoke for a half hour with frequent recourse to the word *"revelloshi"* (revolution), which was absent from my text.

Our next challenge was getting out. It was too high for the aircraft, so we took the auto-ferril—an old Ford with railroad wheels—and went jogging down the single track to Arequipa, whipping around the bends. What if a train comes? ask I. Win a few, lose a few, says the driver in faultless Quechua. On the way, we got stopped and nearly arrested by a local police chief. The charge: refusing to have a beer with him. The Ugly Americans did it again. But you never know about that Indian beer—the Incas' revenge.

PROTOCOL

"The World of Adult Delinquency"

My introduction to the life and times of a protocol officer was abrupt. In 1966 I had been—by President Johnson's appointment and at his pleasure—Executive Director of the President's Committee on Juvenile Delinquency. While attending a gathering of juvenile court judges in New York, I was summoned to the phone. "Jimmy," drawled LBJ, "Lloyd Hand has quit. Will ya do it?" "Quit what, Mr. President?" "Chief of Protocol; will ya do it?" One's hesitancy to enter the unknown is overcome by such a challenge from such a source. "Yes sir," I said, counting the seconds to get to a dictionary. A day later, with right hand raised, I was sworn in by Secretary Rusk, who observed, "You have now graduated from the world of juvenile delinquency to the world of adult delinquency—welcome aboard!"

The word "protocol," I discovered, derives from the Greek words *proto* (first) and *kollav* (glue). Apparently a guarantee of the integrity of some early written agreements was the unbroken seal of glue that held the pages together from first to last. Within a month I was able to refine the definition, to wit: if in a sticky situation you become unglued, you're not cut out for this work.

"It Is My First Time in Your Country"

No sooner had I taken the oath of office as Chief of Protocol than I was whisked off in a State Department limousine to the diplomatic entrance of the White House. A moment later a stretch limo pulled up, and out popped the newly appointed Ambassador Amin Ahmad Hussein of Sudan. We murmured in French to each other

Secretary of State Dean Rusk welcomes James W. Symington as
President Johnson's new chief of protocol on March 22, 1966.

as we entered the House. There we were met by staffers to whom I looked for directions, this being my first time in that part of the executive mansion. Instead of pointing the way, they smiled and stood aside, assuming that I knew where I was going. Not so, yet not wanting to appear hesitant, I walked the Ambassador down a long corridor to a door that looked promising. Taking the arm of my charge, I opened the door. It was a broom closet.

At this point the Ambassador turned and said, *"C'est mon premiere fois dans votre pays"* (It is my first time in your country). He may have thought this was a planned stopover of some historic significance. I explained to him that it was my first day on the job. His nation did not break relations with us until the six-day war with Israel some months later.

"How Many of Our Flags Are Upside Down?"

This bland inquiry was put to me by Britain's Prime Minister Harold Wilson, as the presidential limousine glided into the circular drive leading to the diplomatic entrance of the White House. His reference was to the British flags proudly held by the honor guard lining the drive.

"Surely the Prime Minister is jesting" was my lame and fearful response. "Not at all," said the PM, smiling. "There's one! Why, yes; there's another! And over there, two more!"

The Union Jack consists of the crosses of England, Scotland, and Ireland, superimposed on a field of blue. The variance of thickness of the white diagonal stripes above and below the center defines whether the flag is being flown properly. The thick white stripes should be on the top on the left side, and on the bottom on the right. A number of our fellows had it upside down. The honor guard serves under the Commanding General of the Military District of Washington. But it is brutally clear that, when things go wrong in a state or official visit, that the Office of Protocol is answerable. The buck stops there.

"Not to mind," said our genial guest of honor. "Happens all the time. It is, of course, a signal of distress."

Nor were my troubles over. When we had pulled up to the red carpet, and I had introduced Mr. Wilson to the President, the two stood for an unfortunately extended moment directly in front of one of the upside-down flags. An enterprising photographer recorded the moment for posterity. This was brought to my attention at six o'clock the following morning by a phone call from the White House. "Have you seen the paper?" asked the leader of the free world. "No sir." "Well, get it; I'll hold." Heart in mouth, I padded barefoot across the dewy lawn and scooped up the moistened *Washington Post*. There on page one was a well-focused photo of the two principals standing before an errant flag. The caption—"Oops"—engraved the moment for history. Returning to the phone, I was treated to a surprisingly restrained request to be more attentive to details of this nature.

While I hoped my travails would end there, this was not to be the case. The lead article in the paper's social section described the planned entertainment for the state dinner that evening. Aware that the visit was taking place against the background of sterling devaluation and British withdrawal from holdings east of the Suez, I noted with concern the proposed repertoire for the proud voice of baritone Robert Merrill. His first selection was "I Got Plenty o' Nuthin'"; his second, "On the Road to Mandalay";

Heard and Overheard

his third, "You'll Never Walk Alone," choices all made by the artist. I found myself placing a call to the British Ambassador, Sir Patrick Dean. I asked him if he had seen the morning paper. He had. I then asked if he thought a restructuring of the program might be in order; he would let me know. A half hour later, the Ambassador called back to say, "Not at all; these are all the PM's favorite songs, and he looks forward to hearing them." And so he did, to his own and the President's considerable amusement and to the chagrin of the tattered "Chief." Later that night I penned an alternative version of the lines of William Ernest Henley:

> Out of the night that covers you,
> Black as the pit from pole to pole.
> You may thank whatever Gods you do
> You're not the Chief of Protocol.

"Your Plane, Sir"

In the spring of 1966 President Johnson scheduled a meeting of Asian leaders at what would come to be known as the Manila Conference on the Vietnam War. On arrival at Andrews Air Force Base in Maryland he was taken in hand by the base commander. Preoccupied as he was with the multiple problems of office, LBJ strode along the long line of parked military aircraft. As he turned and placed a foot on the ramp of the nearest C-130, his escort courteously checked his progress and gestured toward a giant plane down the line, the majestic Air Force One. "Your plane, sir," he said, "is over there."

"Son," replied the President "They're *all* my planes."

"The Queen Wouldn't Like It"

Prior to our arrival in Wellington, New Zealand, the first stop on our seven-nation barnstorming tour of allies in the Vietnam conflict, I had been instructed to find hotel accommodations for the President and Mrs. Johnson, who preferred not to stay in the Governor-General's Palace with the demands of politesse that would be made on LBJ's time and flexibility. My job was to explain this to his host the Governor-General of New Zealand, Sir Bernard Fergusson, Baron Ballantrae of Auchairne and of the Bay of Islands, KT, GCMG, GCVO, DSO, OBE.

Having made an appointment with Sir Bernard, I entered his palatial domain and was conducted to an immense parlor adorned with a full-length portrait of the host in his scarlet dress uniform bespangled with decorations. At this point in strode the man himself, every inch as imposing as his resplendent portrait.

"Well, well, well, Mr. Symington, let me say how proud and delighted Lady Fergusson and I are to have the President and Mrs. Johnson as guests in our home."

"The President is most grateful for your kind invitation," I said a bit nervously. "But he feels it is too much of a burden on your household, given the comings and goings of the Secret Service and staff. He has directed me to find quarters in a local hotel."

"Oh, no," bellowed Sir Bernard. "Impossible! The Queen wouldn't like it one bit. . . . No, no, the President and Mrs. Johnson will stay with us!"

When I made my report to my friend Bill Moyers, who was then in charge of LBJ's schedule, he dismissed the idea out of hand. With the impatient air of one who has sent a boy to do a

The chief of protocol routinely welcomes visiting heads of state, such as Mexican President Gustavo Díaz Ordaz, who arrives by helicopter.

man's job, he muttered, "I guess I'll have to tell him myself." "Okay, come with me," said I. Arriving together at the executive mansion, we were ushered into the same grand reception area dominated by the full-length portrait of our host, who stormed in with the same overwhelming exuberance he had greeted me.

"Ah, Mr. Moyers," he said, "I can't tell you how pleased Lady Fergusson and I are to have President and Mrs. Johnson as our guests."

Bill's response, as I recall: "The President and Mrs. Johnson are most grateful."

"*You* Pick the Dang Thing Up"

Air Force One had landed in Wellington, and the jet engines had sighed to a halt when the President emerged from the forward exit to shake hands with the dignitaries. There followed a ritual for which we had been hurriedly briefed by Prime Minister Keith Holyoake. We were standing together when a Maori chieftain, chubby and naked to the waist (save a dazzling array of tattoos), lunged toward us and flung a stick at our feet. The President's eyes narrowed. I explained that it was his part to pick up the stick and show thereby that he came in peace. The chieftain made loud grunting sounds and pointed at the stick. He rolled his eyes ominously, with an occasional nervous glance at the Prime Minister. Disinclined to stoop, the President muttered, "*You* pick the dang thing up." I did so, explaining to the puzzled warrior that I was the President's "Peace Stick Lifter." Relieved, the chieftain hefted his finger-painted tummy back into the safety of the crowd.

The President then decided to shake hands with all the

Heard and Overheard

Maoris, who stood in line with feathers, sandals, and war clubs dangling limply. It had been ages since their tribe had eaten a couple of Captain Cook's men. As I followed along, one of them grabbed me and sang in perfect Beatle-inflected English, "I Wanna Hold Your Hand." So much for the warrior tradition.

"I Call This the Sheep Dip"

Sir Bernard Fergusson was a gracious host at the diplomatic reception. As he led President Johnson to the holding area where guests would gather before being announced and conducted into the great reception hall, he employed a reference to his nation's most notable product: "Mr. President, I call this the sheep dip." The analogy relieved the Texan of any suspicion that the Queen's representative took himself too seriously.

"Symington, You'll Have to Do Better ..."

To the best of my recollection "Agh, Ugh, Aagh" were the sounds emitted in 1967 from the wide-open mouth of Leabua Jonathan, prime minister of Lesotho, a small African Nation and President Johnson's honored guest. Rotund to an advanced degree, he overflowed the chair I proffered him at the President's direction and was making a gallant attempt to respond to the world leader's innocent inquiry, "Are you enjoying your stay in America?" Overwhelmed by the magnitude of that challenge, our stage-struck visitor could not articulate a reply. The President then pulled his own chair up closer, and in the manner of a concerned orthodontist, peered down the mouth of the stricken Chief, as if his looming

Chief of Protocol Symington presents the Emperor of Ethiopia,
Haile Selassie, to President Johnson.

proximity could evoke a response. The Chief's eyes rolled beseechingly at me—my cue to inform the President that the visit was going very well, "thank you, sir." The President sighed, leaned back, stood up, and with a disapproving glance at me, made for the exit to the Rose Garden. I was left to escort my trembling charge to the door and limousine. Returning to view the damage, I was met by the President's longtime aide Marvin Watson, who chided me, "Symington, you'll have to do better with your people."

A state visitor of a different dimension and volubility was the Lion of Judah, Ethiopia's diminutive Emperor Haile Selassie. Arriving with a small white dog in his arms, he disappeared contentedly into the same patient chair that could not quite contain Chief Jonathan, and proceeded to speak without pause in a rapid-fire manner that overmatched the skills of his State Department interpreter. Between the two of them they consumed an hour of the President's time without benefit of interruption, while the little dog dashed about the office, occasionally jumping onto his master's lap. This was a testing time for the leader of the free world, who glanced at me for permission to extricate himself. Interrupting emperors was not in my CV, but I managed to signal the need to wind up the history lesson. This time the President concluded the session with warm expressions of pride and support for the doughty little emperor, as he gently drew him and his canine armful to the exit.

"Get Them Rabbis Off My Back"

The year: 1967. The occasion: Informal visit of President Zalman Shazar of Israel. Scene: the White House Rose Garden. Players: President Johnson and the Israeli President.

It was a pleasant enough day for President Johnson to escort his guest through the glass doors of the Oval Office that opened onto a little terrace overlooking the Rose Garden. Earlier that month, a full-page advertisement in the *New York Times* had called for immediate withdrawal from Vietnam. It was signed by a long list of influential American rabbis. Having settled in adjacent chairs by a table with tea service, the two men were chatting amiably when the President put down his cup, leaned forward, and hovered over his diminutive guest.

"Lemme ask ya sump'n," he said in an offhand way.

"Yes, Mr. President."

"Do you think a country big as ours, with enormous challenges we got here at home and all around the world, should take an interest in the survival of a far-off little old country [Israel] of maybe two million folks?"

President Shazar, getting his drift, replied, "Absolutely, Mr. President. It is the right thing to do, and America does what's right!"

"Well, then," continued LBJ, "what if it was a country, say, of twenty-some million [South Vietnam], threatened by communists? What about that?"

"Certainly, Mr. President, it would follow that America would provide what help she could to such a country."

Leaning back in his chair, and in a voice that shook the latticework, the President thundered, "Then get them rabbis off my back!"

His guest spilled his tea, and it could have been a coincidence, but we never heard another word from that particular disaffected rabbinical source.

"I Am a Semite"

In the fall of 1966 King Faisal of Saudi Arabia made a state visit that involved several scheduled stops. Its success was marred by ravenous press coverage of his offhand response to the question of why companies doing business with Israel were not welcome in his country. The King unfortunately availed himself of a familiar expression, "Those who help the enemy are the enemy," a simplistic formula clearly not intended to apply to Uncle Sam, who he well knew was in Israel's corner.

The message was picked up in a nanosecond by the press and by New York Mayor John Lindsay, who had scheduled a thousand-guest dinner for the King to meet a cross-section of New York society. On learning of Faisal's ill-considered remark, the Mayor observed, "I may have to cancel the dinner." That could spoil a Chief of Protocol's day, so I placed phone calls to two prominent Jewish American leaders, New York Senator Jacob Javits and U.S. Ambassador to the UN Arthur Goldberg. Each assured me he would weigh in at once to keep the dinner on course and, in effect, show the King "what kind of people we are." They tried . . . to no avail.

It then became my duty to inform His Majesty. Arriving at Blair House, I explained the matter to his Equerry, a tall, robed dignitary with a scimitar dangling from his belt. Solemnly he mounted the stairs to the King's chamber. A few moments later he returned, smiling. "His Majesty says dinners are canceled from time to time for many reasons. He will be going to New York and expects to find dinner somewhere."

The Mideast press, less generous, featured wrathful headlines and editorials to the effect that our Mideast policy was made not in Washington but in New York. Mayor Lindsay undoubtedly anticipated adverse political consequences and disruptions that could ruin the King's visit. I remember thinking this might not have been the case had all the players been privy to Faisal's conversation with the President, in which, while acknowledging tensions with Israel, he emphatically disclaimed any intent to resort to arms, hoping rather for diplomacy to secure a just solution to the Palestinian question. Of lesser moment, but significant, was his pledge to broaden women's rights in his country.

As a footnote to this sad tale of Manhattan, I received word from an aide to New York's Governor Nelson Rockefeller that, in light of the Mayor's disinvitation, the Governor's scheduled protocolary call on the King at his quarters at the Waldorf Astoria "would also not occur." Ignoring my protests, he went on to inquire blithely whether under the circumstances there would be any problem were the Governor to attend his brother David's planned luncheon for the King. Marveling at such chutzpah, I said I would put the question to the all-suffering Equerry.

"Certainly," said he, "the Governor can attend his own brother's lunch. Needless to say, should he at any time approach His Majesty, it would be incumbent upon his Majesty to turn his back on him." I conveyed that message, and the Governor lunched elsewhere. What was he thinking?

The King's visit had begun in Tidewater Virginia, at Colonial Williamsburg, to give his party a day to recover from jet lag and their flight across nine time zones. During our carriage ride through the restored 18th-century village to a waiting helicopter, he told me he preferred not to be considered anti-Semitic. "After all," he said, "I am a Semite."

The horses balked some fifty feet from the looming green monster with the spinning rotors, disinclined to take one step further. The postilion in his tricorn hat whipped and urged them on—to no avail. As the carriage swayed and lurched in situ, the King, well acquainted with equine behavior, leaned close and whispered, "It is a mistake to urge an animal beyond his limits. Moreover, to these horses yon helicopter appears to be a huge horsefly. I suggest we dismount and walk." And so we did.

A tragic postlude to the foregoing was to be written in the blood of three contemporary leaders, each of whose inclinations toward peace were aborted by assassination: Israel's Yitzhak Rabin, Egypt's Anwar Sadat, and Faisal himself. Throughout his visit the King stressed the importance of containing the spread of godless communism. "This," he said, "should be the shared commitment of adherents to the 'sky' religions," which he named in order of their appearance on the world scene: Judaism, Christianity, and Islam. In the aftermath of this debacle I checked the "good books" of all three. In one way or another, each expresses the tenet given voice in the Koran: "If a stranger sojourns in your land, you shall not wrong him."

"Oh, *Demi*-TASS!"

While traveling with Secretary of State Dean Rusk to the seven-nation Manila Summit Conference, I was treated to a tale of his predecessor, Dean Acheson. Apparently Secretary Acheson, having concluded some remarks to the foreign press, asked whether there were any questions. A hand went up. "I recognize the gentleman from TASS [the central Soviet news

The chief of protocol and his first lady of protocol, Sylvia Symington,
step out for a state dinner.

agency]," he said. "Am not TASS, am Czechoslovak journalist," replied the aggrieved reporter. "Oh," said Acheson apologetically, "*Demi*-TASS."

"The Genius of Uruguay"

"May the genius of Uruguay which produced *Ariel* guide our thoughts." Thus spoke President Otto Arosemena of Ecuador in his keynote address to the Conference of American Presidents in Punta del Este, Uruguay, in April 1967. As I sat with the U.S. delegation headed by President Johnson, Ariel was a familiar memory; I had learned the part for a grammar school production of *The Tempest*. But Shakespeare was hardly Uruguayan. Who, then, was this "genius" who had usurped "Ariel?

I asked the members of President Johnson's staff. Shrugs. I then went over to the press table where the literati were gathered and put the question to them. "Forget it" was the response of perspiring journalists waiting impatiently for the bottom-line numbers on aid and trade. The opening line of a keynote address seemed to deserve better. Their reaction brought to mind the fellow who was asked, "Which is worse, ignorance or apathy?" and replied, "I don't know and I don't care."

But when my circle of inquiry expanded to a Uruguayan diplomat, the answer came at once. *Ariel*, he told me, was an essay written at the turn of the century by the Uruguayan philosopher José Enrique Rodó, well known to serious students of Latin American literature. Copies were probably available, he said, at the nearest bookstore. He was right. I still have the dog-eared paperback Spanish edition that I bought that afternoon and took to the beach for a quiet read. Speaking over the chasm of years with confidence and wisdom, his Prospero, surrounded by a few admiring students, seemed in fact to be addressing a much wider audience, including generations to come and most particularly our own.

By "our own" I mean the "me generation" of today. "A civilization," wrote Rodó, "acquires its character not from a display of prosperity or material supremacy, but from the grandeur of thought and feeling possible within it.... [We] must begin by recognizing that when democracy is not ennobled by an idealism equally as energetic as the society's material concerns, it will inevitably lead to a favored status for mediocrity."

Heavy-duty stuff, these reflections appear in his *Ariel*, an essay written in 1900—that is, before airplanes, TV, microchips, and iPads—by a twenty-nine-year-old Uruguayan philosopher, who foresaw with clarity and regret the encroachment of "utilitarianism" on the world's technically advanced societies. Thus, while fully cognizant and indeed respectful of North American achievements in political freedom, science, and technology, he urged the youth of Hispanic America not to become "de-Latinized"; to lose, in effect, their identity in a mindless emulation of the North. Hence his suggested comparison of the United States to the insensate and plodding Caliban, as distinct from his romanticized vision of a Latin American culture of beauty and sensitivity implicit in the winged spirit Ariel, which he pleads with his "students" to honor.

Rodó, according to the *Encyclopedia Britannica*, was "considered by many to have been Spanish America's greatest philosopher." Here certainly was a heads-up signal to a high-level

Heard and Overheard

delegation of gringos, presumably seeking common ground with their Latin American counterparts. As Mexico's recently departed genius Carlos Fuentes noted, "the people of North America should understand the political history of Latin America derives from a Latin American reality, not in spite of it." Above the Rio Grande, every school of thought on such questions is on vacation.

"Would You Like a Lift?"

This welcome offer was made through his rolled-down limousine window by Secretary of State Dean Rusk. He had spotted me running full tilt to catch up with President Johnson's motorcade, which had already pulled out and gathered speed at the conclusion of the welcoming ceremony accorded us in Seoul, Korea, the last stop on our 1966 Asian tour. Helping others to their cars, I had become detached from my own as the long line of limos lurched into gear and worked its serpentine way through the some one million people who had gathered in the square to honor the leader of the free world. Most of the happy throng were inclined to chase after the departing cars, so the competition was daunting. But I had the most compelling motivation to keep up, as it was my first day in a city I didn't know all that well.

"I've Decided Not to Help"

In 1966, as Chief of Protocol with responsibility for the welfare of the diplomatic community in Washington, D.C., it occurred to me that diplomats "of color" were not at all in evidence on the rosters of the city's various private social clubs. If club privileges might on occasion be extended to a nonwhite ambassador, they were certainly not available to those of lower rank and their families. Yet these were the very folks whose impressions of American life would inform their entire careers, which could well culminate in high office. Moreover, it seemed timely indeed overdue for an unsegregated country club to be established in the capital area. The World Bank had something of the kind, but its facilities were restricted to the banking community.

I envisioned a club that would welcome junior diplomats and their families and bring them together with colleagues from the corporate and bureaucratic worlds in which they worked. Thus, for example, an African diplomat might enjoy a golf game and a drink with a corporate or government official with related interests. I expected sponsorship funds from U.S. corporate sources. Embassies, by paying a nominal fee, could allocate usage among their staffs.

This would remain only an idea unless and until such a facility could be found or built and the necessary funding secured. In 1968 two remarkable events gave rise to the hope that both these objectives were within reach. First, I discovered a club for sale in Northern Virginia, just seven miles from Washington, D.C. It consisted of about 200 acres, and was known as the River Road Country Club. It had an eighteen-hole golf course, tennis courts, pool, and clubhouse, and was available for a mere $2 million. I immediately made the rounds of major corporate government affairs offices to put the case, or rather the cause, to them. Lacking the "vision thing," they exhibited polite indifference.

Heard and Overheard

Belgian Ambassador Louis Scheyven honors diplomatic tradition and Mrs. Symington, while Deputy Protocol Chief George Abell looks on.

My tentative approach to a few black friends, including Hobart Taylor and Carl Rowan, immediately produced $40,000 in seed money. Placing this fund in escrow in the American Security Bank, I renewed my feverish, though doomed, quest for corporate, foundation, or other support.

A few weeks into the effort, I was approached by a successful Washington businessman. He told me he had heard of my project and thought so highly of it that he would personally finance the entire enterprise. I told him such a gift would certainly constitute a "naming grant" and could not imagine a finer moniker than his for the purpose should he wish it. It was the happiest moment of my two years in the Office of Protocol. The following morning, as I continued to rejoice, I received a phone call from one of the gentleman's sons. He said he thought I should know that his father had always wanted to be an ambassador. Swallowing the lump of anxiety this intelligence produced, I said, as cheerily as I could, that I could not imagine anyone better qualified for such a post—a bit of a stretch, but forgivable, I should have thought, in the circumstances. The caller said he was "leaving that thought" with me.

While neither disposed nor empowered to effect an "arrangement" of such dubious nature, propriety, and legality, I thought I might at least bring the bizarre proposal to the attention of my boss, the unflappable Secretary of State, Dean Rusk. Dismissing the notion as entirely outrageous, he mused, and then recalled that this fellow had at one time been named Honorary Ambassador for the flag raising of a far-flung newly independent island. This recollection prompted Mr. Rusk to make the following suggestion: "Why don't we arrange a ceremony here at the

Department at which I can confer upon this patriot a plaque inscribed appropriately to reflect the gratitude of his country for his services as U.S. Ambassador?"

In a trice I was at a sporting goods store on Ninth Street that produced plaques for the sundry local heroes of basketball, football, and other athletic achievements. Secretary Rusk approved my choice and the inscription, to which he affixed his signature. A late afternoon ceremony was arranged in the State Department's elegant little Monroe Room. The putative donor and his excited family appeared on the dot. Sherry was served, and as we stood around exchanging pleasantries, in strode our Secretary of State, plaque in hand. While family members dabbed their tears, he presented it with an eloquent flourish to its beaming recipient, who responded with gracious words of acceptance.

It was not until the following day that I was made to realize we had misread our man. For on that day, he interrupted my glow of contentment with a phone call in which he asked whether I thought "that little business yesterday afternoon" was a sufficient response to the interest conveyed to me earlier. Once again I took flight from the rigid confines of discretion by blurting, "Why, nothing was further from our thoughts!" This may have been the last straw for a hitherto indulgent Providence, which then prompted our hero to reply with crisp finality, "In any case, I've decided not to help with the club." As nothing greatly surprised our Secretary of State in those tumultuous times, he received this news with a Ciceronian expression that merely conveyed the familiar cry of the human heart: "O tempora, O mores."

For my own part, I was preparing to run for Congress that fall, and having no residual resources or ideas to keep my club plan alive, I returned the money my black friends had advanced. The subsequent years of convivial meetings, family outings, and the infinite permutations and combinations of individual and collective empathy and initiative they could have produced have been forever lost. What conflicts might have been avoided? What enduring friendships struck? As I think back, perhaps a better strategy would have been for Secretary Rusk, immediately and before the filial intercession, to have invited the gentleman to his majestic office to thank him in person for such a splendid, farsighted, and noble civic gesture. Such eyeball-to-eyeball attention at that level might, I say *might* have kept our donor on course without testing the integrity of the process. But history does have an annoying way of concealing its alternatives.

"I Would Have My Ears Cut Off"

Scene: The private dining room at Blair House (the President's Guest House), 1967. Present: Virginia Rusk, wife of Secretary of State Dean Rusk; the Queen of Nepal; Mrs. Kirti Nidhi Bista, wife of the Nepalese Foreign Minister; Mrs. Padma Bahadur Khatri, wife of the Ambassador of Nepal; and Sylvia Symington.

While the Queen was fluent in English, her two diminutive compatriots, Mrs. Bista and Mrs. Khatri, spoke not a word of it. While seated, their feet didn't quite touch the floor. Mrs. Rusk and the Queen opened the conversation with an exchange of pleasantries. The other two ladies remained smilingly silent, despite Sylvia's gallant efforts to engage them with such openers as "Children? How many?" (with a show of fingers). "Four? How nice!"

Having been briefed on this limitation, Mrs. Rusk was relieved at the sight of the State Department's translator Tom Burgess, fluent in Nepalese. Standing in the doorway and preparing to enter, he was suddenly yanked back out of sight by Mr. Haldane, the Chief of Protocol of Nepal, who had not been invited to attend despite the Nepalese requirement that no man may be in the Queen's presence unaccompanied by her protocol officer. The luncheon proceeded under the considerable handicap of two silent, if smiling, participants, legs dangling under the table.

Bidding adieu to the Queen and her ladies, Mrs. Rusk summoned Burgess to account for his absence. Tom explained that no man could be in the Queen's company without the presence of her Chief of Protocol. When asked what the consequences of such a transgression would be, Mr. Haldane stated, "I would have my ears cut off." Mrs. Rusk acknowledged that this could have spoiled the visit.

"Geev Me Zat Wallet"

Among our favorites in the Washington diplomatic corps in the 1960s was France's Chargé d'Affaires, Gérard Gaussen. Handsome, cheerful, and precisely professional, he and his beautiful wife Solange brightened our days in Protocol. His melodious Gallic accent made even his most mundane observations curiously appealing. But etched in our memory was his uproarious account of an incident during his previous service in the United Nations.

Extremely fit, he would start each diplomatic day with an early morning jog through Central Park. One such run produced the following reminiscence:

James W. Symington reviews the Presidential Honor Guard at a ceremony accorded him at his retirement as U.S. Chief of Protocol.

"I was jogging along when fellow from behind boomp me! Ee boomp me! And run away. I feel for my wallet. Gone! I chase de man. I ketch him. I trow him down and I say, 'Geev me zat wallet eemedi- ately!' Ee geev it me. I stuff it een my pocket, and ee run away fast. When I feenish my run, I go home. I go to my room and take out ze vwallet. Eet is not my wallet. My wallet is still on dresser where I left eet. Ooh la la! I run to my car, joomp een and drive to ze address in de wallet. I ring ze bell. Ee open ze door, but when he recognizes me, he cry out, 'No! No!' and slams ze door in my face. I shout to heem through ze mail slot, 'I deed not come to rob you, sir, but to return your wallet.' Ee opens ze door, and we have coffee together."

"I Will Lose My Head"

Life teaches us that the gracious acceptance of a gift is as impor- tant to a relationship as the giving of it. So it is understandable that from time to time such exchanges have become an integral component of statecraft.

This was brought home to me very early in my tenure as Chief of Protocol. Apparently at the outset of our Republic, the viceroy of a North African sultan conveyed the latter's wish to express his friendship by presenting a pair of lions to the U.S. consul for transmission to President Jefferson. When the consul dutifully conveyed the offer, he was advised that the Constitution forbade acceptance of gifts. Informed of this decision, the viceroy said, in effect, "Too bad."

"Why is that?" asked the consul. "Because there will be no further relationship between our countries." "Really?" "Yes, and, albeit of lesser importance, I will lose my head."

"Let me try again," said our consul.

His subsequent report resulted in a hurried acceptance of the lions. Bear in mind that months had to elapse before ocean-born messages could reach their destination—a trying time, I should think, for the participants.

"A Toast to the Chief"

A place at a White House state dinner is well deemed a matter of honor. Accordingly, pressure for invites was not unusual. So I was not entirely surprised to receive a call from the Italian Ambassador, Egidio Ortona, to the effect that the omission of a certain Italian general from the guest list for President Johnson's forthcoming state dinner for Italy's President Giuseppe Saragat was "unacceptable." The State Dining Room seated 120. So we were chock-a-block. Of course as Chief of Protocol I was required to attend, but this pitiful anvil was no match for the hammer of Italian sensitivity. So I ate in the kitchen, keeping a weather ear on the event. Moreover, I was in the best of company, since Mrs. Johnson's aide, Bess Abell, and the Secretary of Health, Education, and Welfare, Joe Califano, had also given up their seats to members of the Roman entourage.

I can now attest that the food, service, and spirit of camaraderie in the kitchen equaled, if they did not exceed, that offered in the dining room. We had a jolly time. That is until Joe, in a burst of enthusiasm, stood up and thrust out his glass in a "toast to the Chief of Protocol." He did so with such a flourish that the contents of the glass, vintage merlot, splashed down the front of my dress shirt, giving me the appearance of an unsuccessful duelist.

By this time the dessert dishes had been removed, and the President was scheduled to rise and toast his principal guest. Nor could he do so without the prepared remarks I had been assigned to hold and hand to him at the right moment. Time was of the essence. The White House Chief Usher, Mr. J. B. West, a benign observer of our revels, without hesitation tore off his jacket and shirt, handing the latter to me as I stripped down to the skin. Buttoning it in a frenzy and retying the tie, I donned my jacket, slipped into the dining room, and placed the precious document into the President's already outstretched hand. After the exchange of presidential compliments, I returned to the kitchen and the raucous plaudits of my dinner companions.

"Never an Answer Like That"

Mankind and its governments have long wrestled with the impulses and proprieties that characterize sovereign largesse. For our part, until 1967 no limit was placed on the value of gifts from foreign governments to U.S. officials, which they could permanently retain in their possession. In that year, Senator William Fulbright of Arkansas, chairman of the Committee on Foreign Relations, held a hearing on his proposal that gifts to be retained should not exceed $100 in value. He arrived at this figure after weighing the diplomatic niceties against the appearance of undue influence on the recipient.

As Chief of Protocol, I was summoned to testify on the proposal. Chairman Fulbright asked whether I thought it was an appropriate sum. My response: "Mr. Chairman, if you think so I think so." Fulbright reared back, turned to one of his committee colleagues (my father), and laughed, "I've never had an answer like that in my life." Thus, while diplomacy dictated the gracious acceptance of any gift, large or small, those in apparent excess of $100 in value were to be turned over to the government or to a tax-exempt entity. Thus the bejeweled gold arm bracelet kindly conferred on Sylvia by the King of Morocco wound up in a display case in the main building of the University of Missouri's St. Louis campus. The accompanying carpet at first adorned my Protocol office and then my Congressional office. Upon my defeat for the Senate, it joined the bracelet. Sic transit imperial largesse.

"A Congressman or Some Other Fool Thing"

President Johnson and I had just bade farewell to Israeli Prime Minster Levi Eshkol and his party at the conclusion of his December 1967 visit to the LBJ ranch in Johnson City, near Austin, Texas. I took the occasion to mention to the President my intention to run for Congress from St. Louis the following year. The President, carrying the woes of the Vietnam War on his back and conscience, along with protestors' cries of "Hey, hey, LBJ, how many kids did you kill today?" settled back in his chair and with a kindly smile said, "Well, I knew you's gonna be a teacher or a preacher or a Congressman or some other fool thing. And I'll campaign for ya or agin ya, whichever you think would help you the most."

He then asked me to delay my announcement until the first of April 1968. I readily agreed, although I would have preferred to get started at once. Thus it was that on March 31, 1968, the eve of my return to St. Louis to make my announcement, I hosted a

200   *Heard and Overheard*

small farewell party for my diplomatic friends at Blair House. At the height of the festivities, someone said, "Hey, the President's on television!" Rushing to the TV set at the far end of the living room, we witnessed Johnson's declaration that he would not seek reelection that fall. He had apparently long selected April 30 as the deadline for announcing his intentions.

Because the Vietnam War was front and center in Americans' minds, his decision derived from his perception of the nature and degree of public confidence in his leadership. It must have been touch and go in his own mind even up to the moment of his announcement, as I learned later from his counsel, Harry McPherson. The President had asked Harry to prepare two drafts: one to the effect he would run for reelection, and the other that he was stepping down to remove the burden of his perceived war-related unpopularity from the ticket and to concentrate his energies on ending the war, undistracted by campaigning. In measured tones he gave the latter.

Despite Vice President Humphrey's gallant catch-up effort to succeed to the presidency, we were headed for the Nixon years.

PART THREE: IN PRIVATE, GENERALLY SPEAKING

Jim pedals the family pedicab, souvenir of an Asian trip, with Sylvia, Julie, Jeremy, and the patient retriever, Brandy.

LEGACY

"My Father Saw George Washington"

This improbable revelation was made to me on a summer evening in 1956 by my ninety-six-year-old great uncle, John Fife Symington of Baltimore. His father, Thomas Alexander Symington—years after the death of his first wife left him with six children—at the age of seventy-two married Angela Stuart, a young lady he'd met in church. Together they raised two more children, including Uncle John.

Their home was located on the road between Philadelphia and Georgetown, a route General Washington frequently traveled. With advance notice of one such journey in 1798, Thomas's father lifted the five-year-old boy on his shoulders to get a better look at our Founding Father as his carriage passed. Uncle John said to me that any country whose entire history could be spanned by just two generations of one family could hardly be considered "old," or, as he put it, "at the end of its tether." "No," he beamed, "we've got a ways to go."

"I Didn't Know They Had Men Like That"

In 1862, at the age of fifty-six, my great-great-grandfather, James Samuel Wadsworth, Republican candidate for governor of New York, left campaigning to others as he assumed the post of governor of the Military District of Washington in the nation's capital. While serving in that post he was called upon to decide the fate of a young Virginia farmer, Patrick McCracken of Spotsylvania. McCracken had been arrested within Union lines and held pending a determination of his status as an infiltrating spy or a private citizen who had strayed into Union territory. Accordingly, he was brought before General Wadsworth, who had the power of life or death over him.

"So you're a spy," said the General.

"No, sir," replied McCracken. "I'm a farmer."

"A farmer, you say," said the General. "Why, that's what I do."

The conversation then turned to the respective growing seasons of the Genesee Valley and the Shenandoah. It ended with Wadsworth's directive to his orderly: "Release this man. He's a farmer, and he may grow something we can eat."

Two years later, General Wadsworth, in the Battle of the Wilderness, was shot from his horse and fell into Rebel hands. Taken to the Confederate command post, he was placed in a hospital tent. The diary of a wounded Union officer who shared the tent records the curiosity of a Confederate soldier, who peeked through the tent flap to see the elderly, six-foot, white-haired Wadsworth and declared, "I didn't know they had men like that."

Some three miles away, McCracken heard that a Union general named Wadsworth was "down." Making a beeline for the Confederate encampment, he secured permission to enter the tent. There he watched as his old benefactor breathed his last. Securing permission, he took the General's body, together with all his effects (save for his binoculars which had been "appropriated") and buried him in a temporary grave on his farm. He then wrote to Wadsworth's widow to say that he had the "remains of your husband" and would keep them safe "until they can be returned to you." Within a few days the General's son and nephew, both Union officers, were granted a pass from General Lee to retrieve the body. General Wadsworth is now at rest in the family plot in Geneseo, New York.

Heard and Overheard

General Wadsworth, Civil War hero and Jim's great-great-grandfather, controls his steed in a heroic posthumous portrait by Alonzo Chappel.

A few years ago, I received a serendipitous phone call from one Terrence McCracken who, believe it or not, was looking for a Wadsworth descendant. Why? Because he knew his grandfather Patrick had been visited after the war by General Wadsworth's son and nephew, who, in gratitude for the consideration shown the General, bestowed a considerable sum of money on the McCracken family, which had resulted in the purchase of local properties including a liquor shop.

Needless to say I invited Terry McCracken, now a deputy sheriff in Leesburg, for a hamburger and milkshake in Middleburg. The meal fortified our drive to the Wilderness battlefield, where we came upon the weathered plaque marking the spot where the General fell. On the way home I invited Terry to attend an upcoming celebration in Geneseo in the General's memory. He came with his wife and took the town by storm. As descendants of Wadsworth's command were to don their Union duds, Terry was told he could wear the gray. Uncomfortable with that notion, he arrived in the outfit of an antebellum dandy: silk top hat, spats, and waistcoat. As you might expect, he was the hit of the day. During the closing reception held in the high school gymnasium, we gave our respective accounts of the events that had brought our ancestors together, two men, I submit, who had been ahead of their time.

"Keeps Me from Getting a Big Head"

My Republican grandfather, James W. Wadsworth Jr. of Geneseo, New York—Speaker of the State Assembly at the age of twenty-seven—subsequently served two terms in the U.S. Senate

(1914–28) and nine in the House (1932–50). A veteran of the Spanish–American War (1898) where he saw how inadequately trained volunteers like himself were, he became a stickler for military preparedness. This was evidenced in the Selective Service Act of October 1940, which he sponsored and which bore his name. The most that President Roosevelt could get out of Congress was a one-year draft. As events of 1941 had begun to shape the world, in August of that year, Roosevelt called on Congress to extend the draft, which was about to expire. In fact "OHIO" (Over the hill in October) was the slogan of the some 600,000 draftees. No admirer of the President, Wadsworth nevertheless supported his request. The vote occurred on August 2, 1941. The debate had been hot and heavy, as members on both sides of the aisle questioned the wisdom of intervening in another European squabble that did not warrant our involvement.

When Wadsworth took the floor, the House was packed. There was a reserve of respect for his views because he had chaired the Senate Military Affairs Committee in World War I, and, as an elder statesman, enjoyed the confidence of his colleagues in both parties. Giving due recognition to arguments on the other side, including Congress's commitment to one year's service, he reminded his colleagues that "Hitler, Mussolini, [and] Tojo [are] controlling the ball, calling the plays and refereeing their own game." Our boys, he said, "are suited up and ready to go." He pointed out that an army is a set of teams, for example, "three men who can take a machine gun to the top of a hill, and hold that position." To break up those teams, he said, would render us vulnerable for a dangerous period. His bill to extend the draft for another year passed—by one vote.

According to my grandmother, on December 8, the Army Chief of Staff, General George C. Marshall, called to say, "Wadsworth, you've saved two million American lives and shortened the war we are about to enter by two years. Thought you'd like to know."

At the 1960 Democratic Convention, its chairman, House Speaker Sam Rayburn of Texas, who had participated in the 1940 House debate, took my brother and me aside to say that in his long career he had heard many speeches that changed members' votes. "But only one," he said, "changed the *result* of the vote. That was your granddaddy's speech of August 1941 on the Draft Extension Act." Its passage ensured that on December 7, 1941, just three months later, we at least had 600,000 men under arms to start the job.

My older brother Tim (Stuart Jr.) and I, both teenagers, were working that summer on Grandpa's farm. He kept a bushel basket on his front porch, full of hate mail denouncing him as a "warmonger" with no consideration for young American lives. Every morning he would reach down into the basket, pull out a few, read them thoroughly, and put them back. Tim, who had the nerve, finally asked him, "Gramp, why do you do that to yourself?" "Well," he said, "I tell you, boys, it keeps me from getting a big head."

Addressing Grandpa's testimonial dinner upon his retirement from Congress in 1950, General Marshall, who had become Secretary of Defense, praised his "priceless and timely contribution to the nation's safety" via the nation's first peacetime draft law. He also reflected on his 1920 Senate measure to preserve the citizen army of World War I, saying: "If Congress had passed the original Wadsworth Bill, I do not believe even a Hitler would have dared provoke a second world war, and without the havoc of that war, there would have been no present menace of a third world war."

"You Could Go; Me They Would Shoot"

The handsome young French Air Force pilot Philippe Bunau-Varilla was the grandson of his namesake, the scheming French engineer who, after Panama's separation from Colombia in 1903, took it upon himself to negotiate a treaty with my great-grandfather, Secretary of State John Hay. This agreement, the Hay–Bunau-Varilla Treaty, ceded virtual sovereignty over the Canal Zone to the United States, and it remained in effect until President Jimmy Carter barely convinced a majority of the Senate to replace it with a version less inimical to Panama's dignity and interests.

In 1962 young Philippe was visiting his mother and stepfather, the French Ambassador to the United States, Hervé Alphand. As we chatted at an Embassy reception I suggested that the two of us might pay a joint visit to Panama "to see what our ancestors had wrought." What had occurred to bring those ancestors together?

After four years of struggle, the French Panama Canal Company, which the senior Bunau-Varilla served as an engineer, had abandoned its attempt to dig a ditch across the mountainous Isthmus of Panama (as they had across the level Suez). At that time Panama was a province of Colombia. Upon the French company's demise, Hay was authorized by President Theodore

At the State Department, Jim poses with the portrait of his great-grandfather, Secretary of State John Hay, by Ellen Emmet Rand.

Roosevelt to negotiate a treaty with Colombia's Chargé d'Affaires in Washington, Tomás Herrán. This treaty draft, approved by the U.S. Senate, was rejected by the Colombian Senate, which preferred to hold out for a larger sum than the agreed-upon $10 million. This rejection prompted TR's outburst, "Those little bandits!"

At this point Bunau-Varilla took the opportunity to visit the President and ask what the United States would do if Panama were to secede from Colombia. According to Hay, "the President received this intelligence with an unmoved countenance," a reaction his visitor correctly interpreted. Notifying his Panamanian confederates accordingly, they "seized the day." Their ensuing declaration of independence occasioned the immediate arrival of Colombian soldiers, who were met by an American military contingent that reminded them of their joint duty to prevent violence in the canal area. The Colombians retreated, scratching their heads, and thus was a new little nation created out of the whole cloth of U.S. imperial interest.

Bunau-Varilla then received the authorization of Panama's first provisional government to open negotiations with Secretary Hay. He not only opened them but concluded them without his principals' approval. When they saw what he had signed, they repaired at once to Washington to seek an audience with TR to achieve a fairer arrangement. They were met on arrival by their erstwhile negotiator, who advised them that any such disturbance of TR's peace could jeopardize the entire business and even stimulate interest in renewing talks with Colombia. It was under such duress that they returned home empty-handed and brokenhearted. Is it any wonder that Señor Bunau-Varilla never found it convenient to return to Panama, or that prudence would dictate his grandson's disinclination to go there with me? Replying to my invitation, he said, "You can go; me they would shoot."

Independence from Colombia naturally inspired the creation of a Panamanian flag. Two hand-stitched silk copies were made of the original design. One went into Panama's archives; the other came to Hay and eventually to me through his granddaughter, my mother. When I learned that the first one had been stolen from the Panamanian National Museum during the overthrow of the dictator Manuel Noriega in 1990, it occurred to me that I was holding a piece of the patrimony of the Panamanian people. So I turned it over to Panama's Ambassador to the United States, Eduardo Vallarino. Two years later, my wife Sylvia and I were invited to attend Panama's Flag Day celebrations as guests of newly elected President Guillermo Endara and to make a formal presentation of the flag, which I did with the following remarks:

Mr. President:

It is my pleasure and honor on behalf of the descendants of Secretary of State John Hay to present to you and to the people of Panama this flag. It is a flag—one of the first two made at the moment of Panamanian independence—hand-stitched by two Panamanian ladies, Angelica Bergamoto de Ossa and Maria Ossa de Prescott, and presented to Secretary Hay by Mr. Bunau-Varilla on the occasion of the signing of the Hay–Bunau-Varilla Treaty at the Department of State, Washington, D.C., on November 18, 1903.

The flag was given by Secretary Hay to his daughter, my maternal grandmother Alice Hay, and her husband Senator James Wadsworth of New York, then by the Wadsworths to my

mother, and finally by my father and mother, Senator and Mrs.
Stuart Symington of Missouri, to me.

Over the past three decades of service in the Department of
State, in the United States Congress and private law practice, I
had observed the efforts of some four Presidents of the United
States to achieve a renegotiation of the original treaty. I also met
many Panamanians in public and private life who were very
desirous of such changes. Mr. Hay himself was quite aware of
provisions in the original treaty which were likely to prove obsta-
cles to normal relations between our countries. Accordingly, after
the successful adoption of the new treaty in 1977, I determined
that it was time for the flag to go home.

Circumstances have delayed this moment of transfer, but I
cannot think of a more appropriate time, or a more auspicious
occasion, to effect it than on Panama's Flag Day. With this beau-
tiful and time-honored flag, Mr. President, comes the heartfelt
hope that the problems of the past will give way entirely to an
enduring era of friendly relations and cooperation between our
two American republics.

Mr. President, to you and Señora Endara, and to the members
of your government here gathered, my most sincere thanks for
your kindness in receiving my wife and me with such cordiality,
and for accepting the repatriation of this hallowed cloth.

For the record, it bears mention that Hay was actually sympathetic to Panamanian feelings, as illustrated by his reply to some
senatorial grumbling. In dismissing suggestions that the
draconian text of the treaty was actually too soft on the little
newborn nation, he wrote, "This treaty is vastly advantageous

to the United States, and one must say with what face one can muster, not so advantageous to Panama. It is a treaty to which a Panamanian patriot could well object."

As indeed they did, and continued to do, until its abrogation by a divided Senate at the behest of President Carter. President Johnson, keenly aware of the danger to the canal itself posed by the hostile nationalism the treaty was engendering, had paid a brief goodwill visit to the country in 1967. The Hay letter, enlarged to billboard size, greeted us on our arrival in Panama City. Then acting as President Johnson's Chief of Protocol, I confess I saw no compelling reason to identify with its author.

"A Couple of Rich Bums"

Tim and I lost our beloved Mother in 1972. Five years later, our Dad met and married the beautiful and gracious widow Nancy Watson, a match that provided us with a warm and delightful stepmother and six dandy stepsiblings.

In 1986 Dad, at eighty-five, invited us to their bayside home in Camden, Maine. One soft summer evening, looking out on the bay, he reflected on his decision in 1945 to leave the presidency of the Emerson Electric Company and embark on a public career that had included five successive federal appointments under President Truman and an ensuing quarter century in the U.S. Senate. Determined at the start to avoid any suggestion of conflict of interest, he had divested himself of the entire portfolio of Emerson stock and options he had been accorded in lieu of a salary when he took over the helm of the strike-plagued company in 1938.

Heard and Overheard

On a sudden impulse that summer night four decades later, he reached for the phone and dialed a call to his aging friend who had brokered the divestment. Their conversation on speaker phone went as follows:

"Craigo, Stuart Symington here. All's well, but I've a question for ya. What'd I be worth if I'd kept my Emerson stock?"

Pause.

"Stuart, are you sitting down?"

"Yeah."

"Your Emerson income would be in the neighborhood of ten million dollars a year."

"Thanks, Craigo. Best to the bride. 'Bye."

Brother Tim broke our slack-jawed silence with the following rueful comment: "You could have thought of your kids."

"Oh, I did," he laughed. "Would have just made a couple of bums out of ya."

"True," Tim said, "but we could have been a couple of rich bums."

GROWING UP

"And You Will Play Third Pig!"

This uplifting designation has sustained me over the perilous years. It was conferred in 1932 by my kindergarten teacher at the Elmwood Franklin School in Buffalo, New York. As you undoubtedly know, each of the three little pigs was tasked to build a home for himself. The first hastily concluded that a house of straw would serve the purpose. The second, only slightly more meticulous, fashioned his of twigs. The third, believing in the importance of a well-constructed permanent residence, set about building his of brick.

The three had barely settled into their respective dwellings when the Big Bad Wolf appeared on the scene. This canny carnivore had no trouble blowing the first two houses down. The frightened occupants managed to flee and run far enough to reach the sturdy edifice of their prudent and fortuitously hospitable friend. A moment later, the well-fanged wolf appeared. Employing the same lung power that had demolished the other two homes, he drew himself up, eyes blazing, and huffed at the house of brick. When that didn't work, he puffed! It is not clear from the record how long he remained huffing and puffing, but eventually a peek out the front window confirmed his frustrated retreat and return to the forest.

All the above was old hat to the assembled five-year-olds, including the three securely nestled under a card table covered with a blanket, which was my house. In the glow of communal pride and congratulations I consumed my share of cocoa and cookies, returning home in triumph. To be chosen to play the third pig was no small matter.

"I'll Take That!"

By 1932 I had turned five and become capable of indignation. I was enjoying my cereal in the kitchen before heading off for kindergarten when my father stormed in, said "I'll take that," and plucked from my grasp the shiny five-dollar gold piece my grandparents had sent for my birthday.

It seems that by order of the government all gold coins were to be turned in. This was deemed one small step in President Roosevelt's struggling effort to mitigate the Depression that was worsening. Further, at that time every household in our neighborhood was contributing one dollar each week to a pot that would be given in its entirety to the neighbor deemed in greatest need. I never learned whether Dad made his summary snatch to comply with FDR's executive order or to ante up for the local kitty.

Little Innocent Lamb

The summer of 1935 was deceptively uneventful from the perspective of a seven-year-old. I was preoccupied for the month of August with a little lamb named Skippy. Skippy's mama had unaccountably rejected her offspring, which was accordingly committed to my care on my grandparents' ample front lawn on their farm in upstate New York. Every morning for the next couple of weeks I administered milk from a bottle to the ravenous little fellow, who practically bit off the rubber nipple. We would then frolic about the lawn in a game of tag.

One day he didn't show up for our session. I thought nothing of it, assuming he had reached an accommodation with his grumpy maternal parent and rejoined the flock. A week later our family dinner was interrupted when my older brother, a seasoned farm hand at age nine, asked me with an innocent smile if I knew what we were eating. "Lamb chops," I said, wondering why Tim would put such a question. "Where," he asked, "do you think they came from?" "No idea," I said. "It's Skippy!" he announced triumphantly.

Ignoring family protocol, I shot to my feet, rushed upstairs, and hid under the bed. It took a great deal of coaxing to get me to emerge and accept the ways of our mysterious world.

"Jimmy!"

I've heard that exclamation countless times, and more often than not in remonstrance. But one instance stands out above the others. As a fifth-grader at St. Bernard's School in Manhattan, I was assigned a minor part in the school's annual presentation of Shakespeare in the auditorium of Hunter College. As the keeper of the jail in which Richard II is confined prior to his murder, I was to bring him his last meal, saying, "Here is thy sup, Sire." The King, suspecting poison, dashes it from my hands and strikes me. On the night of the performance my eighth-grade schoolmate, Robert Nieman, playing Richard, took me aside to advise that he would have to deliver a true blow to make the moment convincing. I acceded readily and could hardly wait for the scene. No sooner had I reached "Sire" than Nieman floored me with a right to the jaw. I crumpled ecstatically into a lifeless lump. The ensuing moment of silence was broken by a piercing cry of "Jimmy!" The voice was my mother's; the laughter the audience's; the chagrin mine.

"You're Late for Lunch"

"Am I right in thinkin' they's a fat gal 'round here?" That question was put to me by a perspiring hitchhiker who had waved me down as I drove my Granddad's farm truck along the road to Geneseo, New York. At sixteen, and newly licensed, I was proud to help a stranger, even an odd-looking one. Rotund himself, he was wearing a multicolored sports jacket, orange trousers, and a porkpie hat pulled over one eye. Breathing heavily, he told me he was with the traveling carnival, had run out of gas, and was headed to town to find a filling station, a ride back to his car, and hopefully a replacement for their "fat lady," who had run off with one of the barkers. I told him our gas station was closed but that I could take him by shortcut to the town of Avon some seven miles up the road. I said that while I knew of no women of his description in or around Geneseo, he could make inquiries all along the way from Avon to Rochester, twenty or so miles distant. With an appreciative grunt as we pulled up at Avon's old Shell station, he kicked open the passenger door, leaned back to hand me a fifty-cent piece, and sought out the proprietor.

Returning to Hartford House, my grandparents' nineteenth-century stucco dwelling overlooking the Genesee Valley, I was met at the kitchen door by their beloved cook of many years, Rilla. Her huge frame filled the doorway as she waved her spatula and scolded, "You're late for lunch, young man!" "Sorry, Rilla, got held up in traffic."

Heard and Overheard

"Stop Trying to *Remember* and Start to *Think!*"

Deerfield Academy had its origins in a colonial charter. When Frank Boyden took the helm as headmaster in 1901 there were but eight boys enrolled. He not only coached the baseball team but had to play on it as well. Early on he hired a promising young math teacher, Helen Childs, at a parsimonious wage. After he noted that she was managing to save money, he married her. Their long, happy life of service was an inspiration to generations of fortunate students.

One day in 1943, I remember, Mrs. Boyden posed a question concerning an algebraic formula that stumped my classmate, who winced and looked to the ceiling as if the answer were there. In her measured, motherly tones, she chided, "Ernest, stop trying to *remember* and start to *think!*" Advice for the ages.

"The Japanese Have Attacked Pearl Harbor"

On Sunday afternoon, December 7, 1941, my Deerfield Academy roommate, Chuck Schmidt, and I were lazily tossing baskets when our English teacher, Bob McCullom, rushed into the gym, shouting the above announcement to no one in particular. Chuck and I looked at each other and said simultaneously, "Where's that?"

We were soon to learn—at that evening's "Sunday Sing," a school tradition that brought the entire student body together, sitting on the floor, hugging our knees, for an hour of hymn singing and announcements. The legendary headmaster, Mr. Boyden, took the occasion to say, "Now, boys, your job is here! When you've learned something you can join up!"

That fall Chuck and I had received permission to attend the Amherst–Williams football game between the two traditional rivals. Chuck's brother Bill, captain of the Williams team, was as gifted a running back as I have ever seen. His freshman year he joined a scrub team to scrimmage with the varsity. Receiving the kickoff, he ran the length of the field for a touchdown. "Wait a minute," said the coach. "Let's try that again." Receiving a second kickoff on his goal line, he wove his way once more into the end zone. Returning to the locker room, he found a brand new varsity uniform folded on the bench in front of his locker.

Chuck was enormously proud of his seemingly indestructible Navy lieutenant brother. Two years later, he was informed that Bill had gone down with his ship, the *Liscome Bay*, a "baby" flattop that had been torpedoed in the Pacific. When asked about his brother, Chuck would only say, "He's in the Pacific."

"You'll Never Go Hungry"

"Tiger" Ted Lowry was an African-American heavyweight contender, one of only three opponents not to be knocked out by Rocky Marciano on his way to the world title, and sometimes called his toughest opponent.

Tiger was a "spoiler," a fighter whose frustrating technique of dodging and deflecting punches prevented his opponent from doing his best work. Tiger agreed to train me at New Haven's Elm City Gym in the winter of 1949. I had biked over to that side of town after being defeated by my classmate Jimmy Hullverson in pursuit of Yale University's lightweight crown. (Our coach, Mosey King, a sixty-year-old former professional

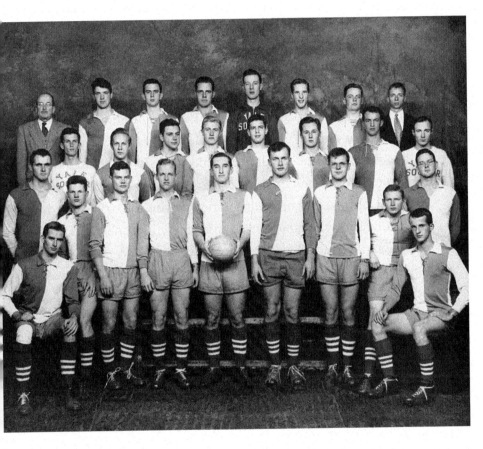

Sporting a cast on an injured knee, Jim sits (left) for the official portrait of Yale's undefeated varsity soccer team in 1948.

bantamweight, did little but fret whether his fighters would hurt each other.)

Accordingly, in search of new secrets to the game, I climbed the rickety stairs of the old gym, a murky loft full of aspiring and perspiring pugilists. Lowry took me in hand for two months of push-ups, light and heavy bag work, rope skipping, and ring strategies. As my intended opponent's style featured roundhouse hooks, it was necessary to fight from a "shell," as Tiger put it, gloves high, elbows in, jabbing the target through the shell. Three weeks into such training I went back up to Yale's Payne Whitney Gym for a second encounter with my redoubtable classmate. The lessons had paid off, and the match (according to the ref) would have resulted in a draw had I not lost my footing, slipped to the floor, and foolishly taken a ten count before renewing the struggle.

The day of my "graduation" from his merciless tutelage, Tiger put his considerable hand on my shoulder and said, "Boy, you'll never go hungry," a compliment that retired my cup. Thus I was prepared and keyed up for a third bout with my old nemesis, again for the 135-pound title. At 129 I was safely within the margin. Unfortunately, he, at 145 on the day of the fight, was obliged to default. History was left panting, and I turned my attention to the glee club. But I shall never forget nor feel anything but beholden to my mentor in the manly art, Tiger Ted Lowry.

Chez Monsieur Renault

After a hiatus (of which more later) I rejoined the Yale class of 1950 and booked passage with two classmates on a refitted troop ship bound for England in the summer of 1949. Earlier that spring, we had dropped in at the Fifth Avenue sales office of the Renault company to look at cars, the smaller and cheaper the better. The winning candidate, costing $800, was a tiny member of the Renault line called the Juvaquatre. The plan was to tour England and Scotland by train, cross the Channel in an excursion boat, and then train to Paris, where we would pick up the preordered car, drive down the Loire Valley into Italy, and back up by way of Austria to Amsterdam, where we would book our homeward passage and sell the car.

Arriving in Paris after touring a somber England barely recovering from the war, we took a cab to the Renault outlet on the Champs Élysées to fetch the car we had bought and paid for in New York. To our surprise, the floor manager, with a shrug of the shoulder, apologized, "So very sorry, we have no cars." We pointed out that they should at least have the car we had purchased. "Non! There has been a strike, and no cars delivered!" Devastated, we returned to our *pension*, where I had an idea: I would go to the factory myself and fetch one. Agreed. So I entered the Paris Métro for the first time in my life. Having looked up Renault in the phone book, I determined which of the maze of red, yellow, and blue lines on the Métro map would take me to that address. Boarding the designated train, I sat back and watched the scenery go by. Eventually, we reached a suburban area with tree-lined avenues. Curiously, the address I had naively noted featured a towering iron gate that opened onto a cobblestoned courtyard leading to a huge mansion. An old woman, scrubbing the stones, looked up and ran off.

Nothing daunted, I approached the giant carved oaken double door and knocked firmly. It opened, revealing a young man in a well-tailored suit. *"Que voulez-vous?"* he asked politely. *"Je veux mon voiture!"* (I want my car!), I blurted. My accent must have betrayed my preference for English, as he smiled and said, "Do you know where you are?" Persisting in some sort of French, I said, *"C'est l'usine* [factory], *non?"* "Not quite," said my amused interlocutor. "You have come to the home of Monsieur Renault."

Ignoring my confusion, he beckoned me to enter and follow him down a corridor lined with sporting prints. On reaching his office—he proved to be Monsieur Renault's private secretary—he dialed a phone and gave an order to the other end of the line. Putting it down, he laughed, "You have your car. I admire your courage." With that, he summoned a limousine, which conveyed me in high fashion some distance to the actual factory, where, amid dozens of idle workers munching on submarine sandwiches, a company official led me to what appeared to be the sole remaining Juvaquatre on the lot, which I boarded and drove away without further ceremony. Returning to the *pension* after some hair-raising encounters with Parisian traffic, I proudly presented the prize to my companions. "How did it go?" they asked. "Not bad." We then proceeded to put some three thousand miles on the sturdy little vehicle before selling it in Holland for almost twice the purchase price. New cars were scarce in Europe.

"Yes!"

It may not have been the right answer, but it was a welcome one. On a June evening in 1952, while standing on her piano bench so she would remember the circumstances, I proposed marriage to Sylvia Caroline Schlapp, a St. Louis belle I had pursued for two

Heard and Overheard

nerve-racking years. Before the wedding we were summoned before Father Sant, the priest at St. Michael's Episcopal Church, a block from Sylvia's home. For some reason he took the occasion to ask, "What do you two like to do together?"

Taken aback, we managed to come up with some innocuous activities like paddle tennis, poetry reading, music and movies.

Letters from Camp

Many years later our son Jeremy, age nine, in his first letter home from summer camp, wrote, "The reason I haven't told you the names of my friends is I have none." Our eleven-year-old daughter Julie's first such letter conveyed a similar observation. Reflecting on her social life, she wrote, "I have made nine friends, all of them dogs."

"He's Not Thinking; He's Talking"

Years ago, as I was jabbering away to Sylvia on some Subject of Great Importance, the phone rang. She picked it up. Apparently the caller asked for me but said not to disturb me if I was deep in thought. Looking over at me, she said, "No, he's not thinking; he's talking."

Home is where you hang your head.

MARINES

"When We Saw We Were Down to You..."

Upon graduation from Deerfield Academy in June 1945, I went directly on to Yale for its "accelerated summer session," part of the vaunted V-12 Program organized to compress college curricula from four to two years, rendering graduates free to enlist in one of the armed services. Toward the end of June a Marine Corps recruiter gave an inspiring speech on the campus, which determined me, at seventeen, to get my father's permission to enlist at the close of the freshman term in early August. Arriving August 9 at the Marine Corps Recruiting Station in Bridgeport, Connecticut, I took the oath administered by a muscular master sergeant. I also took the occasion to ask him about the mysterious bomb reported to have been dropped on Hiroshima just four days earlier. Looking disdainfully at my 128-pound frame, he explained, "Son, when we saw we were down to you, we went with everything we had."

Indeed, history's second and, thus far, final nuclear weapon was dropped on Nagasaki that very day. Let it be the last!

"The Motliest Bunch..."

By 1945 my brother Tim, an army corporal, had served in both theaters of the war. Not looking forward to his returning assurance that he had won it by himself, I took the opportunity a month before my eighteenth birthday to enlist in the Marines. A week later the Japanese, taking note, surrendered. This took some of the glamour from my decision, one which nevertheless provided an educational opportunity denied in other centers of learning.

A marine recruit's first day in boot camp was rendered

memorable in a number of vivid respects, beginning with frequent assurances that he and his fellow new arrivals were as useless a crowd as ever walked the earth. An unceremonious visit to the barber, and consequent abrupt shaving to his pink scalp of locks once carefully combed to lure the opposite sex, contributed to that impression. This was done with the victim's back to the mirror. The operation complete, he was twirled around to view his shame. At that point, stripped naked, he was obliged to run a gauntlet of screaming graduates of the process, their function being to hurl epithets while flinging his assigned garments at him. He then joined the "motliest bunch ever to assemble," this being the candid assessment of the drill instructor (DI). For openers, this granite-jawed worthy serves up a reminder that events will prove warranted, namely: "as far as you people are concerned, the sun rises and sets in my a—."

After the passage of a mere twenty-four hours, the recruit is able to confirm the prediction. In quick order, he and his comrades, regardless of background and circumstance, are reduced to the lowest common denominator of self-esteem, only to find it handsomely restored fourteen weeks later, when, assembled in good order on the base parade ground, they receive, directly from the commandant, the Marine Corps emblem, an anchor across the world, and pin it proudly on their barracks caps.

"OFLCD"

That was the 20/20 line of the eye chart I had to read to pass the Marine Corps physical. The examining medic instructed me to close one eye and read it. I knew from experience and previous exams that my left-eye vision was normal, but the right eye was weak, 20/120 to be exact. So with my right eye closed, I read the line with ease. The doctor then told me to "close your other eye," which I did. "Now read it," he said. Although the line itself was now a blur, my limited powers of retention were sufficient to enable me to repeat it—OFLCD—and thus pass the exam.

The early weeks of boot camp were marked by instruction in "snapping in," that is, assuming the proper positions for firing at different distances—five shots each, in positions of diminishing stability: prone at 800 yards, sitting at 500, kneeling at 300, and standing at 200. The day we fired "for record," rain and fog swept over the firing range. As gun sights are designed for the right-eyed, I couldn't quite make out the bull's-eye until that last position. Ah, there it was! At this point, the sergeant pointed out I had done so poorly at the greater distances that I would have to put all five in the center to pass. As flunking meant "riding the range" (scrubbing the base stoves with steel wool all night for a week), I was motivated to make all five count—and did.

A possible consequence of the effort was the eventual restoration of normal vision in my right eye.

"This Is a College Man Diggin' a Hole"

Early in boot camp we were introduced to the "entrenching tool" (folding spade) that could be strapped to a knapsack. As you might suspect, it could be used to dig a foxhole. On reaching the testing ground, our DI, Sergeant Held, asked innocently whether any of us had ever been to college. Without reckoning the possible consequences, and thinking imprudently that honesty might be the best policy, I raised my hand. "Well, that's *terrific*," the Sergeant beamed. "Now you just take this here shovel and dig, and I want the rest of you people to pay attention, 'cause this ain't no ordinary guy diggin' a hole, it's a *college* man!" As the laughter subsided, I flailed away, determined to become more circumspect about my checkered past.

"About the Right Proportion"

A Marine master sergeant was minding his own pleasure at a bar frequented by service personnel, when a young Army recruit approached with unsteady gait. Poking his finger at the old vet, he said, "You know, every time one of you guys goes into battle he's got an Army division on one side, a Navy flotilla on the other, and an Air Force squadron above." The seasoned old leatherneck seemed to calculate a moment before quietly replying, "Yep, that would be about the right proportion."

"I've Been Watchin' Ya"

In 1975, some thirty years after boot camp, I was at work in my congressional office when my secretary asked whether she should put through a caller who identified himself as "Held." Hardly believing my ears, I took the call.

"Hello?"

"Held here."

"Sergeant Held?" I shouted, snapping to attention.

"Yes sir."

"Well, where are ya? Come on over!"

"Can't do it; catching a train. Just wanted to give you a call. Tell ya I've been watchin' ya. You're doin' alright."

"Sarge! Sarge!"

But he'd hung up. Semper Fi!

MUSIC

"East or West of Broadway"

In 1919 Prince Serge Obolensky, a major in Czar Nicholas's defeated army, carved his way through the victorious Bolsheviks to freedom. Settling briefly in Paris, where he became leader of its Russian community, he gathered up a number of émigrés, set off for New York, and married John Jacob Astor IV's daughter. His patrician bearing, noble lineage, and managerial skills were a decided asset to the Astor family's chain of hotels, including the Sherry-Netherland, which rises majestically near the corner of Fifth Avenue and 59th Street opposite the venerable Plaza, where horse-drawn carriages continue to take tourists on tours of Central Park.

Serge and my parents became close friends during the roaring thirties, when New York nightlife sparkled on into the wee hours. "Supper clubs" abounded. One of these, the Place Pigalle, held an evening of amateur entertainment to raise funds for the poor in the Depression year of 1934. My mother was one of the participants. After one song, the club owner offered her a job for $1,000 a week. My father's reaction: "Hey, Eve, that's more than I make; go for it!" Her father, Congress-man James Wadsworth, had only one question, "Is it east or west of Broadway?" Apparently Broadway was the western limit of seemly activity. The nightclub was a block east, so therewith began Mother's four-year career as a chanteuse in Manhattan's premier hotels, the Plaza, the St. Regis, and the Waldorf-Astoria. The last of these earned her a Hollywood offer in 1939, which she declined in order to accompany her husband and two wayward boys to St. Louis, where Dad

Composer and muse: newlyweds Jim and Sylvia make music in 1954;
she was a music major and timpanist at Sarah Lawrence College.

assumed the presidency of the then struggling Emerson Electric Company.

This was the past which served as prologue to my mother's suggestion—when I left for law school in New York—that I pay my respects to their dear friend of her singing days. In the interim, Colonel Obolensky, having at the age of fifty enlisted in the OSS during the war and parachuted into Sardinia to contact the underground, had returned to the States and donned his tuxedo anew to resume his overview of the Astor holdings. A month after I had begun classes at Columbia Law School, I found a moment to visit. Welcoming me to his table, the Colonel asked if I "took after" my mother in the matter of music. I said I had sung in school and college glee clubs.

"I'd like to hear you," he said.

"When?"

"Tomorrow morning at 9 o'clock, right here."

Cutting my 8 A.M. class on evidence, I beetled by subway, bus, and shank's mare to the hotel, where I found the Colonel. Having descended from his penthouse apartment in a silk bathrobe, he was sipping coffee by the bandstand. Bandleader Emil Coleman's pianist, Freddy Jaegels, who was to prove both mentor and friend, was at the keys. "What would you like to do?" he asked. I chose Mother's signature song, Rodgers and Hart's "My Romance." "Why not?" said Freddy, and with a dazzling array of introductory chords, lifted and launched me into the song. The brief silence after the last note was broken by the Colonel's matter-of-fact challenge: "When can you start?"

Opening in January 1951, I lived an invigorating double life until graduating into the real world.

"If I Talk Roshin to Heem, I Keel Heem"

The speaker's name was Yasha Nazarenko. Six and a half feet tall, barrel-chested, with a mournful Slavic face lined by years of sad memories, he had a laugh that could suspend conversation within a hundred feet and a frown that portended mayhem. His looming presence was a comfort to his fellow émigré and employer, Prince Obolensky. It was good to have a Yasha to handle "situations" in the Sherry-Netherland's popular Carnaval Room.

I played two half-hour performances a night in the Carnaval Room, which was decorated in full czarist splendor, and featured stag heads protruding from the red-velveted support columns. Between shows I had the opportunity to study my law books in a convenient single room on the seventh floor. I now can confess that I preferred to hang out with the guests or to take a breather in the pleasant company of the hatcheck girl at her station. I was so engaged one evening when down the velvet stairs stepped a figure familiar to me from news photos: a short fellow with white hair that stood straight up, as if he had touched the wrong wire. It was clearly Andrey Vyshinsky, Prosecutor General under Stalin and now Soviet Ambassador to the United Nations. Together with his solemn wife, he had mistakenly come down the stairs from the hotel's first floor to the nether tier, which housed the Carnaval Room.

With an uncertain look in my direction he spoke, *"Je cherche l'ascenseur."* I could have told him where the elevator was and probably should have. But knowing that Yasha was a "White" Russian, I pretended not to understand him. Shrugging and gesticulating to indicate the need for backup, I sped out of the area, discovered Yasha tuning his balalaika, and told him there was a gent outside he might

Heard and Overheard

like to see. Yasha rose, placed the instrument carefully down, and strode into the reception area where the disoriented visitors were waiting. At the sight of Vyshinsky, Yasha—I believe the expression is—froze. The thoughts that must have roiled in him made him seem even larger and more threatening. *"Que voulez vous,"* he said in his basso profundo. The unmistakable Russian in his French, and his high-cheekboned countenance being enough to identify his origins, Vyshinsky retreated a pace, eyes fixed on Yasha, and repeated his request timidly. With a sweep of his giant hand, Yasha indicated the recessed area that hid the elevator. Then, in a voice of thunder, as if pronouncing sentence in a capital case, he declared, *"ICI L'ASCENSEUR."* Vyshinsky, fully aware of his predicament, eyes fixed on his erstwhile countryman, reached behind to press the button. When the doors opened, he and his terrified wife backed in.

After they had made their escape, I asked, "Yasha, why didn't you talk Russian to him?" Still trembling, Yasha replied, "Jeemy, if I talk Roshin to heem, I keel him." Thank heaven for the language of diplomacy. Yasha then explained that he was the only member of his family who had survived Stalin's purges. How thoughtless it was of me to put my good and kind friend to such a test. He assuaged my remorse by returning to his balalaika and asking me to join him in a lusty rendition of the gypsy song *"Chto Mne Goryeh?"* (What do I care?)

"God Bless America"

If Mother Russia's maternal instincts under czarist rule did not extend to her Jewish children, America was the principal beneficiary of their understandable desire—in Tennyson's words—"to seek a newer world." Vivid examples of our good fortune in this respect included Israel Isidore Beilin, born in Russia in 1888, and Jacob Gershowitz, born in New York a decade later to Jewish Russian immigrants. As Irving Berlin and George Gershwin, respectively, they enriched our store of popular music beyond measure. While Gershwin's cerebral music ranged from elegant pop ("Stairway to Paradise") to the neoclassical ("Rhapsody in Blue"), Berlin's, by turns romantic ("Always"), playful ("Cheek to Cheek") and distinctly patriotic ("God Bless America"), occupies a special place in America's heart. Knowing of his lifelong happy marriage to my mother's cousin, Ellin Mackay, I was inspired to celebrate his 100th birthday on May 11, 1988, by assembling a score of former congressional colleagues on the Capitol steps for a lusty al fresco performance of "God Bless America." America was certainly blessed by the decisions of the Gershowitzs and Beilins to make their homes here.

It's worth noting that Russia saw the error of its ways in one regard. A few years ago I attended a stirring ceremony at the Russian Embassy at which bemedaled Jewish veterans of the Russian army were honored for their part in the Great Patriotic War.

"Miss Otis Regrets"

Among my extracurricular activities during my first year at Columbia Law School was the study of voice and guitar. The latter brought me together with Chauncey Lee, a black guitarist who had his own radio show. He introduced me to the Guitar Society, which brought together devotees of the instrument ranging in proficiency from beginner to professional. We met in a Greenwich Village loft once a month, sitting in a circle as a guitar was passed around and playing it to the level of our skills when our turn came. Preeminent in the group was Josh White, a genius on a twelve-string guitar that under his touch exploded in rhythm and melody. He smiled indulgently when I told him that I had begun a stint at the Sherry-Netherland.

A few nights later the Carnaval Room's bouncer sidled up to me between shows to whisper, "There is a black fellow named Josh at the door who says he knows you." Racing through the lobby, I found him patiently cooling his heels. I escorted him to a table, bought him a drink, and we visited until show time. Among the numbers I sang with guitar was Cole Porter's "Miss Otis Regrets," the bittersweet account of a wronged woman headed for the gallows after shooting a faithless lover. When I finished the set I looked again for Josh, but he had left. A month later he made a hit recording of the song.

"Give da Kid a Cahd"

One night in March 1951, I had completed my second set at the Carnaval Room and was heading back to the Columbia campus when Henry the bouncer approached and, pointing to two men in dark overcoats standing by the door, whispered, "These guys want to see ya." "What's this?" I thought as I approached the pair. One of them said, "You got a card?" "Yes," I replied, "I have American Express and a driver's license." "You funny?" the larger and more intimidating of the pair inquired. The other interjected, "Union card." "Union card?" I repeated. "Yeah." "Well, I guess not," I confessed. "Do I need one?" "Yeah." "How do I get it?" "You gotta see Mr. Petrillo." "Oh?" "Yeah." "When?" "You be in his office tomorrow, 9 A.M."

The next morning, skipping classes, I appeared at 9 A.M. at the door to the office of James Caesar Petrillo, president of the American Federation of Musicians. The office, the size of a recital hall, was empty except for a heavyset, bald-headed man seated like a Buddha at the far end. "What d'ya do?" he said to open the conversation. "I sing," I replied. "Okay, sing!" he commanded. One of his deputies, seeing my guitar, pulled up a side chair for me. Well aware that Mr. Petrillo was a labor leader, I told him I would like to sing a song about a famous worker, John Henry, the "steel drivin' man" who died after defeating a steam drill, the device that would put him and his fellow hammer-swinging laborers out of a job.

"Yeah, okay" said Mr. Petrillo.

As I sang the last line of the song, "Lord, he was a steel drivin' man," Mr. Petrillo turned to his associates and said, "Give da kid a cahd."

"Play Ball!"

One doesn't hear a great deal about godparents these days. Perhaps they've gone out of fashion. I was lucky to have one in the person of my mother's cousin and cherished friend Joan Payson. Cousin Joan was a lady of enveloping warmth and sparkling wit. Amply endowed physically, she was a commanding presence in any company. A devotee of both baseball and the underdog, she bought the New York Mets and rooted for them with such fervor that her ad lib appearances in their pregame locker rooms kept the players on their toes, towels at the ready.

Her other passion was opera. A member of the Board of the Metropolitan Opera, she had a balcony box that commanded a view of the terrain. One evening's performance of *Aida* that we attended was late in starting—so late, in fact, that murmurs of disapprobation filled the hall. After some twenty minutes, my beloved godmother rose and, leaning against the railing, bellowed, "Play Ball!" The laughter had barely subsided when the curtain rose.

"That Was Very Nice"

On a spring night in 1952, I had just completed a set in the Carnaval Room when the maître d' pulled me aside and pointed out a couple in the back, "He wants to see you." I recognized the man, noted photographer Cecil Beaton, whose studio I had visited per instructions of the editors of *Town & Country* magazine, which was doing a story on supper club entertainment. As I made my way to the table I tried but could not see the lady's face, hidden as it was beneath the broad brim of her hat. "I want you to meet my date," said Beaton. At this the lady lifted her head to reveal the exquisite features of the heroine of *Ninotchka*, the movie classic I had seen twice. This was Greta Garbo. She gave me one of those smiles for which men throw themselves on their swords and then said with that endearing

Swedish accent, "That was very nice." The best I could come up with on such short notice before retiring to my corner was, "Thank you, Ma'am."

"The Third Whistler"

On a day in May 1967, during my stint as chief of protocol, I was assigned to escort an Asian dignitary on a private trip to New York. Reeling from the rigors of shopping, he chose to spend the afternoon in his suite at the Plaza Hotel. Thus released, I contacted my old Yale classmate Sascha Burland, a gifted musician, who had become a successful television writer and producer. As fellow members of Yale's triple quartet, the Whiffenpoofs, during our senior year we had sere-naded everything that moved and a few that couldn't. During my first year at Columbia Law School, we shared a one-room flat on the West Side with our classmate Harry Thayer, then an editor with *Newsweek*, destined to become U.S. Ambassador to Singapore.

Sascha, having been scheduled to record a TV commercial that afternoon, invited me to attend the session. The job at hand was to produce the soundtrack for an Alka-Seltzer spot. It depicted a tired motorist with a nagging family and headache to match. He stops at a filling station, where the sympathetic attendant gives him a bubbling Alka-Seltzer. Quaffing it, he drives off smiling, oblivious to the continuing tantrums of his unpleasant children. As his headache subsides, the background of hitherto jarring sounds becomes a gentle three-part whistle. But stay! The third whistler had not arrived. Costly studio time

At a USO benefit for the March of Dimes in 1965, Jim helps a young performer after her turn upon the stage.

was a-wastin'. Could I, *would* I, Chief of Protocol of the United States, provide the third whistle? Ask not! Alka-Seltzer had done much for me; it was a chance to square the debt. And I still carried my old union card. Taking no more than twenty minutes, this bit of extracurricular moonlighting produced checks for seventy-five dollars each month for the next five months. The lead whistler was pleased. "Buddy," he said, "let me know if you ever need work."

"Not Enough to Hurt My Pickin'"

During my father's 1964 campaign for his third Senate term, we visited his old friend Tony Buford on his farm near Possum Trot in Iron County, Missouri. The beautiful rolling country, capped by the mountain named for generations of our host's family, inspired *An Evening on Buford Mountain*, a collection of folk songs that Buford arranged for me to record in St. Louis. Then and now, the wellspring of country music was tucked in the Missouri Ozarks. The session brought me together with Lee Mace and his Ozark Opry Singers.

Prior to their arrival at the recording studio, I prepared lead sheets for such reliables as "I'll Fly Away," "Wayfaring Stranger," "The Ballad of Jesse James," "Go Tell Aunt Rhody," and the like. Before I could pass them out to each performer, Lee spoke up. "What this fer?" Surprised, I asked a foolish question: "You read music, no?" "Not enough to hurt my pickin'" was his cheerful response.

So it went hour by hour and song by song. I would first sing the number with guitar or a cappella. Lee and his boys would simply listen. We would then take it from the top, and record each number in order. The session lasted into early evening. I had booked hotel accommodations for the group, which they politely declined. Not disposed to spend even one night in the "wicked city," as they put it, they packed up their instruments and boarded their bus back to Springfield, Missouri—God's country.

"All Education Begins with Music"

It may well have been in the spirit of this observation by Plato that Washington's Junior League inaugurated an experimental program of music instruction at the inner-city Harrison School several blocks from the Capitol in 1966. As a former member of the League, Sylvia volunteered to teach music to the fourth grade. The class of seventy-five students had been divided into three tracks: fast, medium, and slow, based on their perceived levels of general learning. Some of them were twelve years old.

By "music" Plato had in mind rhythm as distinct from melody, and the Harrison youngsters were up to the challenge. Equipping each track with a triangle, tambourine, drums, zither, and guitar, Sylvia introduced her classes to a variety of rhythms and melodies. In November one of the regular teachers interrupted a rousing rendition of the Thanksgiving Hymn by taking her aside and admonishing her for presenting her students such lines as "He chastens and hastens his will to make known," words "they could not possibly understand." Sylvia was also criticized for illustrating rhythmic variations

After performing at the British Embassy, Jim meets Prime Minister Margaret Thatcher and her guests, President and Mrs. Reagan, in 1987.

with a recording of Stravinsky. "These kids," she was told, "never heard of Stravinsky. They're into Leadbelly." Happily, these objections were overruled by the school's dedicated principal, Marguerite Selden.

Within a few weeks, the performance levels of all three tracks in all subjects increased dramatically. Such was the influence of a daily dose of music. Sylvia continued to teach her classes until my transfer to the State Department required her full-time participation in our diplomatic life. I brought my guitar to her farewell gathering and sang with them. One of the youngsters, a ten-year old girl, took her hand and asked, "Must you leave us"?

"Ask My Wife"

As I had sung western ballads for then Senator Lyndon B. Johnson's campaign for the presidency in 1964, he may have thought I knew something about music and musicians. In any event, he placed me in charge of selecting orchestras to play at his inaugural balls in January 1965. Familiar as I was with a few of the named orchestra leaders, I prudently sought the help of my old friend Peter Duchin, who, like his famous father Eddie Duchin, had become a renowned pianist with his own orchestra. Peter not only accepted the invitation to play but provided his manager, Otto Schmidt, to help me choose the others. Together we selected Count Basie, Meyer Davis, Lester Lanin, Duke Ellington, Gene Donati, and my St. Louis bandleader friend Russ David. For this invaluable assistance, I let Peter choose his venue, Washington's Sheraton Hotel.

Despite a light snow falling, I rode a bicycle from one venue to another to check on the various parties. On reaching the Sheraton, I found Peter, like the character Schroeder in *Peanuts*, bent over a Steinway and pounding out "Just One of Those Things." A woman of certain years was leaning on the piano and looking dreamily at Peter, who was totally absorbed in his art. Gazing at him, she gave vent to her feelings as follows: "I'd like to go to bed with you." Without missing a beat, Peter, pointing to a smiling lady sitting atop the piano, replied politely, "You'll have to ask my wife."

"Can We Sign You Up for a Two-Week Gig?"

This pleasant offer was made in the spring of 1967 by the proprietor of the Cellar Door, a cozy nightclub nestled on the corner of K and 31st Streets in Georgetown, Washington, D.C. On Monday nights the management invited amateur singers and musicians to perform for the patrons.

One such evening, with Sylvia off in Missouri, I thought it might be fun to take my guitar to the club and get in line with the other hopefuls. Four of us were stashed in a backroom until called upon. When my number came up, I took my place on the barstool provided and sang two ballads, "Greensleeves" and "John Henry." It was like old times in the Sherry-Netherland during my law school years. Returning to the holding room, I was approached by the proprietor with the referenced offer. I thanked him but said I was an out-of-town visitor on my way home to Missouri. I didn't tell him that I had a regular gig—as Chief of Protocol.

"He Heard You"

Having served six years as a congressman on the Health Subcommittee of the House Commerce Committee, I sought out hospitals and infirmaries during my 1976 Senate campaign. At the Children's Hospital in Kansas City, a nurse led me to the bedside of a black teenager who had been shot in the spine. Paralyzed from the neck down, he lay perfectly still, eyes open. I asked the nurse whether she thought he would like a song. "I'm sure he would," she said. For some reason I chose "The Streets of Laredo." Halfway through it I saw tears come to his eyes. I choked up and couldn't finish. "You should be very pleased," she said. "He heard you."

RACE

"We Don't Serve Your Kind"

This was the icy reminder of a prim little waitress in Tucumcari, New Mexico. In June 1943 brother Tim and I were heading for our summer jobs on the Rain Valley Ranch near Sonoita, Arizona when the train broke down and we were told to find lunch in town. One passenger was a young black soldier, trim in his uniform with campaign ribbons. He had stepped off the train and with the other passengers walked across the tracks to the lunch counter. Some twenty of us were in line for service including this decorated young veteran. When he reached the head of the line, the waitress, without looking up, said, "We don't serve your kind." At fifteen I had no idea what she meant. My brother explained.

As the soldier turned to leave, I said, "What do you want? I'll get it for you." At this the entire crowd glared at me. I had said something unpardonable. The soldier smiled and said, "Now don't you go gittin' in trouble with these good folks." He then went around back, as he'd been told, to the kitchen entrance. No longer hungry, we left, wondering what he thought about the America he was defending.

"You Don't Belong Heah"

In 1953, my second year at Columbia Law School, I took tap dancing, jujitsu, guitar, and voice lessons while singing in nightclubs and getting married. The last of these initiatives required a change of residence from the $100-a-month, three-bedroom Greenwich Village apartment I had shared with two fellow Yale

On the campaign trail in 1968, Jim addresses members of the
International Ladies' Garment Workers' Union.

graduates. Because my wife, Sylvia, had a semester to complete at Sarah Lawrence College, we began life together as tenants of a campus dwelling. This required a commute by train from Bronxville to 125th Street, Morningside Heights, and then by subway down to the 116th Street campus.

One afternoon, with no classes scheduled, I decided to return on foot to 125th Street and the train to Bronxville. The day I picked for this excursion was marked by a huge demonstration on the Columbia campus in protest of apartheid policies in South Africa. Those were the last white people I would encounter on my trek across Harlem.

What I did see and hear were the colorful sights and vibrant sounds of another world, which, despite evidence of poverty and despair (not unlike those in parts of the Village and the Bowery), conveyed a joyful atmosphere of purpose and self-confidence. I was particularly struck by the sight of a large white temple topped by a banner bearing the name of "Daddy Grace," a leading local evangelist. As I walked by, Daddy himself, robed and sandaled, appeared at the gilded entrance to welcome a large gathering of his flock.

I stopped at a nearby bar, ordered a beer, and surveyed the scene. At this point an elderly gentleman approached and said in a kindly manner, "Boy, what you doin' heah?" I explained I was on my way to the 125th Street station. "Well," he said, "You be gittin' along now...'cause you don't belong heah." I thanked him for his consideration, cloaked as it was in a rebuke. With the angry shouts of Columbia students still ringing in my ears, I thought how much easier it was to inveigh against apartheid abroad than to tackle it at home.

"We Love Our Negras"

This observation was made by a University of Mississippi student at a small gathering scheduled to hear me out as Attorney General Robert Kennedy's representative during the integration crisis of 1962. It was a challenging time for the school authorities, the students, the teachers, the entire town, and, needless to say, Mr. Meredith himself, the agent of change, who moved through the scene with stoic demeanor. A few days later I accepted an invitation to address a local Lions Club lunch, also attended by Ole Miss students. During my subsequent visit with them in their off-campus house, I was invited to consume a roasted squirrel, including the brain. "Must I?" I asked. "Yep, it's the first thing ya gotta eat." "No exceptions?" "No, suh!"

There being no escape, I plunged the glutinous little white ball well past my taste buds as far down my throat as I could. "He did it!" they yelled. "The Yankee did it! Damn!" "Now wait a minute," I said. "I'm from Missouri, a border state."

At the insistence of my hosts, who made it clear that "we don't water our drinks," I quaffed a tumbler of un-iced bourbon before we got to discussing the reasons for the federal presence in their normally untroubled community. Among the numbing comments made during the ensuing discussion, the most memorable was that of an earnest undergraduate. "Sump'n' ya'll ought to know," he said. "We love our Negras." This reassuring claim was modified by the answer given to my next question, as to why they would object to schooling with folks they "loved." "Ya don't understand," said the spokesman. "We don't love 'em that way. We love 'em different."

I said perhaps we should take "love" out of the equation, and

Heard and Overheard

simply accept the notion of an equal opportunity to learn. Having providentially brought my guitar along, I sang a few lullabies before staggering back to my cot in the school administration building. Returning to Washington, I was summoned to the Senate office of Mississippi's John Stennis. Expecting a dressing-down, I was relieved by his explanation for the summons. "I just want to thank you," he said, "for the way you talked to my people."

"You, Suh, Represent a Tyranny"

As unrest continued at the University of Mississippi, I visited local churches in Oxford, to see what contribution to reason could be expected from that quarter. Some clergymen declined to see me at all. One Episcopal minister had tried to calm the crowd at the Lyceum building before being rendered hors de combat by a brick. But the most remarkable response to my tentative suggestion that a church might weigh in on God's side was made by the pastor of a temple of fundamentalist persuasion. I was prepared to discuss aspects of the problem when he blurted, "You, suh, represent a tyranny!" (the federal government). When I countered that "tyranny" might better describe the state government's treatment of the black community, he did not avoid the implication, muttering, "It's better to have a lotta little tyrannies than one big one."

They're Not Americans

In 1962 drive-in restaurants along America's roads were usually segregated. This was a norm that went unchallenged until an African ambassador, driving up to New York to represent his government at the United Nations, was denied service on a federally controlled highway. The incident was highlighted in a *New Yorker* magazine cartoon depicting a robed and turbaned African diplomat about to be ejected by a restaurant employee, who is admonished by the manager as follows: "It's all right, he can come in; he's not an American." As RFK's aide, I joined the State Department's troubleshooter, Deputy Assistant Secretary Pedro Sanjuan, to notify all restaurants along the federal highway system to desegregate or lose their licenses. Restaurants located along most major highways were not long in lifting racial restrictions.

"We Will Get to These Matters in Our Own Way"

These words, defiantly uttered in blunt Afrikaner fashion in 1980, proved more prophetic than intended. They were spoken by Frederik Willem de Klerk, then a member of the South African cabinet, whom events would shortly propel to the helm of his country's government. Invited to his office in Pretoria, I had just related certain changes in South Africa's governance that I took to be mandatory before the United States would lift the economic sanctions it had imposed as punishment for South Africa's racial policy of apartheid.

The exchange with de Klerk was occasioned by a fact-finding trip to South Africa with Sylvia and my law partner, George Smathers. Our law firm had been contacted by Abe Hoppenstein, a Jewish lawyer from South Africa, whose government had instructed him to secure counsel to provide advice and guidance during the country's inevitable transition from apartheid rule. At

Heard and Overheard

Sylvia Symington visits with Madame Garba, wife of the Ghanaian ambassador, and her son, at a reception for diplomatic families.

that time I knew very little about South Africa other than that my great uncle, Adelbert (Del) Hay, newly graduated from Yale, had been dispatched in 1899 by his father, Secretary of State John Hay, to serve as U.S. consul in Pretoria during the Boer War. He conducted his office so deftly that he not only enjoyed the full confidence of the Boer government but, through his solicitous efforts on behalf of British prisoners of war, earned a commendation and a memorial silver cigar box from Queen Victoria.

The changes I presented to de Klerk included freedom for neighboring Namibia, the cessation of interventions in Angola and Mozambique, and, of most importance, the scheduling of an all-parties conference on the future of South Africa that would establish majority rule in that nation of 25 million black people and 4 million whites. These were the points stressed in earlier visits with my friend and former colleague New York Congressman Steve Solarz and one of America's outstanding black leaders, Congressman Charles Diggs of Michigan, chairman of the Subcommittee on African Affairs of the Foreign Relations Committee. At Chairman Diggs's suggestion I also called on Randall Robinson, president of TransAfrica, an institute dedicated to the establishment of just governance throughout the African continent.

Our law firm's subsequent efforts on behalf of de Klerk's rocky but resolute course included drafting a suggested constitution for the country based on our federal model, which would have established majority (black) rule with protections for the minorities (white, colored, and Indian). This idea didn't make the cut, as the South African government's initial proposal for change provided for three separate houses of parliament: one for

Heard and Overheard

the "Africans," one for Indians and coloreds (mixed bloods), and one for whites, which would have—guess what—the power to veto initiatives by the other two. Events happily overtook this quest, as South Africa in July 1992 emerged "free at last."

"On My Way to Jail"

President Johnson's fixation on Vietnam blurred but could not erase the accomplishments of his Great Society programs. One such was the creation of a President's Committee on Law Enforcement and the Administration of Justice. Another, related to it, was the Committee on Juvenile Delinquency and Youth Crime. The importance he attached to this problem was reflected in the caliber of the giants appointed to head each of the three responsible departments: John Gardner (Health, Education, and Welfare), Willard Wirtz (Labor), and Nicholas Katzenbach (Justice). As Executive Director of the Juvenile Delinquency Committee (which met but once), I reviewed the following transcript of a recorded interview of two inner-city youngsters:

Edward, fourteen, and described as "hopeless" by his school, was asked to tell about his life. His response: "Summers are the worst time, drinking, cussing, stabbing people, having policemen running around most every day. In wintertime they don't come out because the whiskey store is closed, and they can have no argument, nor get drunk and start fighting, 'cause it's cold."

Asked what he would do if a TV camera came on his street, he replied: "I would like my neighborhood to be real nice, and not a whole lot of people around there and fighting, fussing, police be

*always running around there. If they were making a movie around
there I would gather all the people up around our street and tell
them that I would like to see y'all best manners when the studio
come and film our street. So they come and say that's a nice neighborhood. After that ... all the people will forget.... They'll go to
drinking, cussing, fighting, shooting people ... police be running all
around again."*

*Wendell, sixteen, a neighbor of Edward's, compared their
neighborhood to a Maryland suburb. "I was being rode through
Maryland. They was pretty yards, you know, they keep the yards
clean."*

*"Where were you going when you were 'rode' through Mary-
land, Wendell?"*

"On my way to jail."

Values and hopes from the mouths of babes.

"What Can We Do for These Kids?"

The Junior Citizens Corps was founded in the 1960s by residents
of one of Washington, D.C.'s poorest neighborhoods. Its purpose
was to enlist drifting youngsters into social and athletic
programs that would absorb their interest and energies and steer
them clear of gang mischief. My Congressional colleague,
District of Columbia Delegate Walter Fauntroy was a star graduate of the program.

While working for Bob Kennedy, I agreed to chair the program
and track its progress. One evening at our headquarters in Southeast Washington, I showed a David Brinkley documentary film to

Heard and Overheard

the assembled toughs. It depicted the barrio in Peru where I had opened a Food For Peace school lunch program for Lima's destitute children. Their appearance, haunted expressions and undernourished bodies caused one husky young fellow to say,"What can we do for these kids?" A noble concern, I thought, in one neglected child for another a world away.

"I Just Don't Relate to These People"

This was the surprising revelation of a black friend and Justice Department colleague, whom I had invited to my evening session with the young footballers. Later, over a sandwich, he said, "You know, I couldn't have done what you did tonight."

"What do you mean?" I asked.

"I grew up in a Park Avenue apartment," he said. "We had a doorman and elevator boy. I just don't relate to these people."

"Oh sure you do," I said rather too quickly, in the naive assumption that race necessarily defined everyone's comfort zone.

"Jobs, Man!"

That's what he said, the tallest of the some twenty young men languidly leaning on parked cars at midday on the main street of Kinloch, a community located under the flight path of airliners thundering in and out of Lambert Field, the airport serving St. Louis. You knew you had entered Kinloch because the county paving ended.

My visit the fall of 1968 was prompted by the fact it was located in a part of St. Louis County that I would represent if I were elected to Congress, a neglected area that included the now sadly famous city of Ferguson, Missouri. Approaching the youngsters I identified myself as a hopeful candidate. "Yeah," said the tallest, "What you goin' do for us?" A good question which I ducked by asking in return, "What do you think you need?" "Jobs, man!" said the self-appointed spokesman. "What kind of jobs?" "Construction, man. Whenever there's a public buildin' goin' up, like a Post Office, Whitey comes, bangs on the shingles, takes his paycheck and goes home. We could do that stuff, but we just watch on the corner. Cop comes and tells us to move, so we go to another corner."

Our conversation was interrupted by a screech of brakes and a thump. We turned to see a boy of seven or eight, lying twisted on the road; nearby the old truck that had hit him. He was twitching and shivering. I took off my jacket on the run, and draped it over him. His mother pushed through the gathering crowd and cradled his head. My campaign volunteers in their red-white-and-blue straw hats stood aside as a police car pulled up. Two white officers emerged and questioned the distraught truck driver. They had already called for an ambulance, but none came. After some thirty minutes we prevailed on the officers to take the boy and his weeping mother to the nearest hospital. When the squad car pulled away, the tall fellow said "If it'd been me, I'd be lyin' there yet."

As these young Americans dispersed I could not help but wonder what they thought of "their" country, and of their neighborhood in the little suburban city of Ferguson. The level of despair and sense of abandonment moved me and my District Assistant, Jim Brown, to call on the National Guard—not, indeed, to keep order as in the 2014 killing of Michael Brown, but to repair the community infrastructure. We arranged to bring army engineers into Kinloch one weekend a month for over six months during which they tore down decrepit, rat-infested houses to make room for replacements. To secure the latter we persuaded HUD to provide a $10 million grant to finance new housing for the displaced residents.

The subsequent deterioration of the area, highlighted by the Michael Brown incident—the death of an unarmed black teen at the hands of a Ferguson police officer—validates the doleful comment of the 19th-century liberator, Simon Bolivar: "with my revolution I have ploughed the sea."

RELIGION

"... As a Hawk May Circle"

While my attendance at worship services has been irregular, years ago I was intrigued to hear about a handsome and ancient sanctuary in the Scottish lowlands. Dating back to Norman times, Symington Parish Church is one of the oldest church buildings in Scotland. Its name—the name of both parish and village—is an elision of Symon and town: or Symon's Town. Family lore has it that the first American Symingtons hailed from here, and further, that the eponymous gent who founded this hamlet was a brave vassal of the great Scot, Robert the Bruce. According to legend, Symon performed valorous deeds for his liege lord, who became the first King of Scotland and consequently rewarded his loyal comrade-at-arms with a royal grant of land, a tract "as large as a hawk may circle in a day."

"Where's God?"

"Where's God?" This theological inquiry was raised on Easter Day 1960 by our three-year-old son Jeremy, at the top of his formidable lungs amid the hundreds of hushed worshippers in the great nave of Washington's National Cathedral—which we had told him was "God's house." He took a little off its profundity by a quick follow-up question put with equal vehemence, "Where's the Easter Bunny?"

"The Best of Both Religions"

My London-based boyhood schoolmate Prince Azamat Guirey, himself a Muslim, asked me to serve as godfather to his newly born daughter, Selima. Honored by the thought, I nevertheless questioned whether it was in the Islamic tradition. "Not at all," he said jovially. "I just want her to have the best of both religions." Taking my duty seriously, I purchased a copy of the Koran and inscribed it to the new arrival. Realizing that I might be considered off the reservation on this one, I consoled myself with the reminder that Judaism, Islam, and Christianity all stem from Grandpa Abraham, who might be excused for shaking his head at our endless squabbles. Moreover, I was moved to wonder how many of my fellow Christians had familiarized themselves with the parts of the Koran that chronicle the virtues, miracles, and ascension of the prophet Jesus.

A related instance arose during my tenure as Chief of Protocol. In April 1966 I was tasked to prepare for the state visit of the Shah of Iran. My first reaction was to pen new lyrics to "April Showers" ("April Shahs"). My next was to advise the White House on an appropriate state gift for the eminent Muslim leader. My suggestion was a copy of the first American edition of *The Alcoran of Mahomet*. Printed in 1806 in Springfield, Massachusetts, it claimed to have "faithfully translated into English" a French version of the original Arabic text. It had been among the books I inherited from my Grandfather Wadsworth. Before heading to Blair House to present the gift, I perused for the first time the publisher's one-page apologia "To the Reader," in which he absolves himself of responsibility for the book's "blasphemous" content. Needless to say, I hastily replaced this literary time bomb with a book of American poetry.

Meanwhile, back in the world, we might take note that half of its occupants subscribe to none of the Abrahamic faiths. The half that subscribes does so despite Alexander Pope's gentle

Heard and Overheard

admonition, "Know then thyself, presume not God to scan; / The proper study of mankind is Man." Nice try, Alex.

"Don't You Know Any Jewish Songs?"

Morris Shenker, the most prominent criminal lawyer in St. Louis, had been put in charge of a 1956 gala celebration of Irish and Israeli fashions at Famous-Barr, a leading department store. In preparation for the event, he asked me to sing for the gathering: "Not just your Irish stuff! Don't you know any Jewish songs?" This was a daunting challenge until I came across a rousing example performed by Harry Belafonte. From his inspiring recording, I learned the tune and lyrics to "Hava Nagila" just in time for the occasion. That and "Danny Boy" were part of a memorable evening of cultural camaraderie.

Not a Good Question

During his term as the United States Representative to the United Nations Security Council, Senator Warren Austin, a Vermont Republican, asked the following question—more rhetorically than wisely, perhaps: "Why can't the Jews and Arabs resolve their differences in a truly Christian spirit?"

Think of the Trinity

A trip in South Africa to counsel the government on needed constitutional change featured one unforgettable cloudless Sunday in April 1980. Cape Town's mighty Episcopal cathedral,

St. George's, was filled, every seat taken, when a young minister stood to address a congregation whose racial composition mirrored that of the nation itself. Pausing a moment to scan our faces, he began his sermon. "My text today is a simple one," he said. "It derives from the concept of the Trinity: Three in One; that is the Father, Son, and Holy Spirit: separate identities, but merged in one Godhead." He then asked if this wasn't, in fact, a lesson to be learned. "We have grown too accustomed," he said, "to seeing ourselves through the lens of our ethnicity rather than that of our humanity ... a trinity, if you will, of black, Indian, white, or some combination thereof; in effect, one people." As he spoke the entire congregation began to hold hands. Many wept. As we emerged smiling into the bright Sunday air, the very day seemed to radiate hope. Hard decisions lay ahead, recriminations, angry exchanges, and retributions, but no one present at that service could have come away without confidence in the future.

"In God We Trust"

The Founding Fathers were of one mind in their determination that no religious tests should define citizenship, much less eligibility to serve in public office. By adopting Article VI of the Constitution, whereby "no religious test shall ever be required as a qualification to any office or public trust under the United States," and by the First Amendment thereto that "Congress shall make no law respecting an establishment of religion, or prohibiting the free exercise thereof," the Founders registered their determination to break from mankind's history of religious wars

Heard and Overheard

and punishments related to religious practice and preference. Yet an implicit recognition of a higher authority, or accountability, is stamped on the concluding line of our oath of office, "so help me God," also in those words chiseled on the frieze above the House floor: "One Nation, under God, with Liberty and Justice for all."

Not only does our coinage proclaim "In God We Trust," but accountability to higher authority is manifested in the Presidential Prayer Breakfasts that bring together Congressmen and Ambassadors from across the world. These begin with a nondenominational prayer and message from the President in person or by proxy. In 1977, as a member of the organizing committee for President Jimmy Carter's first breakfast, I mentioned the anomaly that the musical entertainment had always been provided by all-white groups such as the Mormon Tabernacle Choir. I suggested it was time to integrate the program. My committee colleagues were supportive of the idea but didn't know any black choruses. Did I?

Indeed, I did. While in Congress I had visited a Baptist Church in St. Louis that featured the Legend Singers under the baton of Kenneth Billups, a choral conductor of the first rank. The committee, taking my word for it, commissioned me to schedule them if I could. Billups was delighted but pointed out the need to finance their travel and accommodations. I had no difficulty in corralling McDonnell Douglas, Monsanto, and a few other kind corporate sponsors. The Legend Singers were a sensation! My reward was to be invited onstage to join them in singing "It Takes Time to Know a Country," which Sylvia and I had written the year before.

It takes time to know a country,
Time to see the land,
Time to meet the people,
And time to understand.

Time to know your neighbor
On the other side,
Time to learn to labor,
In the vineyard of his pride.

Time to watch the reaping,
Tell the wheat from chaff,
Find the reaper weeping
And learn what makes him laugh.

For this great road we're walking,
Has many a pit and bend,
Who can tell for certain
Just where the road will end?

We know it's full of danger,
So walk it hand in hand.
It takes time to know a country,
And time to understand.

"Trust in God"

Toward the end of World War II, a formidable group of German scientists developed the pilotless V-1 and V-2 rockets, armed with devastating warheads. Chief among the rocket designers was Wernher von Braun, who, at war's end, providentially chose

Heard and Overheard

to come to the United States despite Soviet efforts to secure his services.

In 1973, as a member of the House Space Committee, I flew with him on a NASA plane to witness an Apollo launch at Cape Canaveral. During the flight we discussed the implications of man's limitless curiosity and whether we were on a course chartered by ourselves or some unfathomable power. At this point I left the track of propriety and asked whether he believed in God. I was addressing a man of science, who might be expected to put his trust in the proven. "Congressman," he said, "I could not even get up in the morning and go about my day without belief and, yes, trust, in God."

INDEX

Pfc. Symington embraces his grandmother Alice Hay Wadsworth,
daughter of a Secretary of State and wife of Congressman, in 1945.

Index

282

About the Author

James W. Symington was born on September 28, 1927, attended schools in New York City and St. Louis, Missouri, then prep school in Massachusetts. After serving in the Marine Corps, he entered Yale College where he studied history and sang in the Glee Club, graduating in 1950. Attending Columbia Law School, he married Sylvia Schlapp and returned to St. Louis as assistant city counselor before entering private law practice. In 1958 Ambassador John Hay Whitney engaged him as his assistant at the embassy in London. A series of jobs in Washington followed, including deputy director of President Kennedy's Food For Peace program, administrative assistant to Attorney General Robert F. Kennedy, and director of the President's Committee on Juvenile Delinquency. He was named Chief of Protocol by President Johnson in 1966.

In 1968, he was elected to represent Missouri's Second Congressional District, eventually chairing subcommittees on Space Science and Applications; Science, Research & Technology; and International Cooperation. After four terms in Congress, he co-founded the law firm Smathers, Symington & Herlong, which represented good causes in venues worldwide. Having studied Russian and traveled widely in that venerable country, in 1992 he helped found the American-Russian Cultural Cooperation Foundation (ARCCF). He also served as director of the Atlantic Council and as director of the Library of Congress's Russian Leadership Program.

He and Sylvia, parents of two grown children and grandparents of five, live in Washington, D.C., and Middleburg, Virginia.

Illustration Credits

All images are from Symington family collections and published courtesy of author except for the following:

Bachrach Studios, page 2

City News Bureau, Inc., pages 27, 52

William L. Klender, *Baltimore Sun,* page 186

Peggy McMahon, pages 61, 256

Dev O'Neill, pages 35, 66

Abbie Rowe, White House Photographs,
John F. Kennedy Presidential Library and Museum, Boston, page 18

Stan Wayman, *LIFE* Editorial Services, page 202

John Hay Whitney and Betsey Cushing Whitney Papers,
Sterling Memorial Library, Yale University, page 136

Wide World Photos, page 78.

HEARD *and* OVERHEARD: *Words Wise (and Otherwise) with Politicians, Statesmen, and Real People* was designed by Robert L. Wiser in Silver Spring, Maryland. The book is composed in Sentinel, created in 2004 by the Hoefler & Frere-Jones digital type foundry in New York for use in book typesetting as an expansion of the historic Egyptian-style Clarendon fonts. The original Egyptian types of the early 1800s were so named because of a popular mania for all things Egyptian during the time of the Napoleonic conquest of North Africa. Robert Thorne's Fann Street Foundry in London was one of the first to introduce these exotic square-serifed, fat-face display fonts for use in posters, broadsides, and handbills. The style proved to be a huge commercial success and soon spread to America, contributing in part to a proliferation of political campaign graphics, among other printed ephemera, that appealed to the imagination of the voting electorate well into the twentieth century.

CPSIA information can be obtained
at www.ICGtesting.com
Printed in the USA
LVOW01*1723091115

461718LV00002B/5/P